HOW TO WRITE A SONG

(EVEN IF YOU'VE NEVER WRITTEN ONE BEFORE
AND YOU THINK YOU SUCK)

HOW TO WRITE A SONG

(Even If You've Never Written One Before
and You Think You Suck)

ED BELL

Bell, Ed
Book : How to Write a Song (Even If You've Never Written One Before and You Think You Suck)

Library of Congress Control Number: 2019910879

ISBN 978-1-7333750-0-9 (Paperback)
ISBN 978-1-7333750-1-6 (eBook)

First published September 2020
New York City

Cover image by Dark Rider on Unsplash

CONTENTS

OK Cool, Let's Write a Song: How This Book Works xi

Part 1: Find a Great Song Idea 5

Part 2: Choose a Lyrical Hook (or Title)....................17

Part 3: Write the Chorus Lyric................................25

Part 4: Write the Chorus Chords, Melody and Groove..........45

Part 5: Write the Verse Chords and Groove 129

Part 6: Create a Verse Masterplan

       and Write the First Verse Lyric 141

Part 7: Write the Verse Melody and Create a Verse Build...169

Part 8: Write the Second Verse Lyric

       and Start Putting Your Song Together...181

Part 9: Add a Bridge 199

Part 10: Add an Intro and Outro 215

Congrats – and What's Next 227

Appendix 1: 21 Great Song Ideas for Getting Started 235

Appendix 2: Chords, Chord Notes

       and Guitar Chart Cheatsheets.........239

Appendix 3: Verse-Chorus Structure Cheatsheet 249

ABOUT THE SONG FOUNDRY

At The Song Foundry it's our mission to share great songwriting ideas with the world. At thesongfoundry.com we publish articles about songwriting, host free videos on various songwriting topics, and offer Skype songwriting coaching worldwide.

Connect with us online to find out more:

thesongfoundry.com

youtube.com/TheSongFoundry

facebook.com/TheSongFoundry

twitter.com/TheSongFoundry

OK COOL, LET'S WRITE A SONG: HOW THIS BOOK WORKS

OK COOL, LET'S WRITE A SONG

Once upon a time, there wasn't a song.

Then, sometime later, there was.

"How the $&%! did that happen!?" you might ask.

* * *

How *do* you write a song? It's a great question.

Should you start with the first verse? Should you start with the chorus? Should you start with a chord progression? Should you start with a melody or a rhythm or a groove or a title or a deep psychological need to write to fix your broken heart?

And honestly, the answer is yes.

And yes.

And yes.

And yes, yes, yes, yes and definitely, if it helps.

In other words, like most great questions, 'how do you write a song?' is a great question without a single answer.

You can start writing a song pretty much anywhere you like – and as long as you keep going until the whole song is finished, it's all good. In fact, one of the reasons songwriting is so rewarding and so challenging – and one of the reasons there are so many different songs in different styles – is that there are hundreds or even thousands of different ways to write them.

But wait, is that it? Did I really bring you here to tell you that you can write a song pretty much however you like?

No, it's not. And no, I didn't fill a 300-page book with the single idea 'Do what you like, champ!!'.

See, the thing with songwriting is that every song ever written is really just someone's – or a group of people's – answer to the question 'what should a song be?'. It's just their best, smartest, most personal answer – based on their tastes, their experiences, their opinion – to what a song should be.

And in the same way, this book is just my best, smartest, most personal answer to the question 'how do you write a song?'. It's just my best, smartest, most personal answer to what the most helpful but fun and down-to-earth songwriting book should be. And specifically, it's just my best, smartest, most personal answer to what a book called *How to Write a Song (Even If You've Never Written One Before and You Think You Suck)* should be.

Is it the only answer? No.

Is it a smart, logical answer? Absolutely.

Is it an interesting, inspiring, practical, engaging, versatile, powerful and – most importantly – 100% beginner-proof answer that basically anyone can follow? Well, I'll let you be the judge of that, but yes, I really think so.

In other words, yes, this book is about an inspiring process that anyone with some basic experience with a guitar, a piano or a DAW (a Digital Audio

Workstation, like Logic, Ableton or GarageBand) can use to write a song – even if you've never written one before and you think you suck.

We'll talk through a logical, step-by-step process you can use to build every part of a new song from scratch. And – as you'll find out – we'll do it in a way that'll teach you a ton about how songs work, so if you already have some songwriting experience you should find this book useful too.

But as I said, if you're completely new to songwriting we'll also do it in a way that covers everything from the ground up. So again, literally all you need to get started is to know how to play three or four chords on a guitar or piano, or be able to find your way around your DAW of choice. We'll cover everything else.

And if you don't read music, that's OK too. Honestly, learning to read music, even at a basic level, is a really good investment for any songwriter to make – even if you only want to write lyrics. But if you don't read music – and plenty of songwriters don't – as we work through we'll talk about ways to record or write down what you create without using notation.

I've also made audio recordings of all of the music examples in this book so you can hear them as well as see them on the page. The music examples start cropping up from Part 4 onwards, but if you want to download all the tracks in advance, just go to **thesongfoundry.com/how-to-tracks**.

So, in short, I'm going to break down one powerful and versatile songwriting process into ten different parts. I'm going to talk you through the practical nuts and bolts of how to put a song together. I'm going to try my best to demystify the songwriting process in a way that anyone can understand, and if you stick with me, I'm going to transform the way you look at songwriting for good.

And sure, there are people who think songwriting can't be taught. Who think being able to write songs is a talent you either have or you don't.

Luckily, those people are wrong. Kind of.

Because while it's true songwriting can't really be taught – at least, not in the way you can teach someone to drive a car or speak German or calculate the length of a hypotenuse – songwriting can be *learned*.

With the right tools, principles and techniques, you can get smarter and faster at putting songs together. And you can get better and bolder at using those tools, principles and techniques to answer the question 'what should a song be?'. And in short, that's exactly what this book will help you do.

But before we get started on this process for real, we should talk a bit about how this process works – what it is, what it definitely isn't, and what you can do to get the most out of working through it.

FIRST THINGS FIRST: THIS ISN'T A SONGWRITING METHOD

This book is a lot of things. And we'll talk about some of them soon enough. But first, let me set the record straight on a few things this book is not:

It's not a cucumber shaped like the Chrysler Building.

It's not an apology note to everyone I was rude to as a teenager.

It's not every ninth word of the Geneva Convention put together into a surreal abstract poem.

And – most importantly of all – it's **not** a songwriting formula or method.

Come to think of it, the first three were probably pretty obvious. But we should talk about the last one, because it's at the heart of how this book works, and why it's probably different from anything else you might have read about songwriting.

You might have heard of some of music's well-known methods. There's the Kodály method for learning singing and musicianship. There's the Suzuki Method for learning an instrument and ear training, while learning how to be a good person (genuinely). Then there's the rhythm method, which sounds like it's something to do with percussion but actually – no, wait, that's something else.

But seriously – music has tons of well-established methods that break down different aspects of music theory, musicianship and/or learning an instrument in an easy and ultra-accessible way. And that's great.

The trouble is, songwriting doesn't work like that.

See, when it comes to learning to sing or play an instrument, there's already a roadmap. And there's a really clear goal – to perform a piece of music as accurately as possible. So you spend hours and hours developing and refining your skills so you can recreate that piece of music as accurately and as convincingly as possible.

But in songwriting, there's no roadmap. You have to create it.

You're not reacting to or recreating something that already exists – you're creating the thing in the first place. And that changes everything.

That's why songwriting methods or formulas – even if they're helpful in the short term – can only take you so far. They give you a box to create in. They give you lines to draw between. But one day, if you decide you want to create something, you know, *outside* that box – or give yourself your own lines to draw between – what then?

In other words, sure, I could come up with The Ed Bell Method® or The Song Foundry Formula™. And it might help you write one song.

But would it help you write ten songs?

Would it help you write a song you're really proud of?

Would it help you feel genuinely more creative?

And would it help you feel more *alive*?

Probably not.

That's why songwriting can't be taught – at least, in the conventional way – but it can be learned. The key to becoming a good songwriter is to learn to think for yourself, try things your way, make mistakes, learn from those mistakes and keep going until the song you're working on is finished.

And that's why, honestly, a strict method or a formula is the last thing you want as a songwriter – and why this book is going to give you something much better.

It's why this book is going to help you think, not just copy. It's why this book is going to help you create, and not just follow. And it's why – even if you're familiar with some of the ideas in this book already – we're going to look at those ideas in a way that may well be completely new to you.

To explain, let's talk about four key ideas that make this book different.

[1] This book is a *process*, not a method or a formula.

As you know, this book is just one process – a series of logical, easy-to-follow and easy-to-rely-on steps and techniques for writing a song. It's not the only way, it's not even the 'right' way – it's just one smart, reliable way of creating a finished song time after time.

And because this book is about a process, not a method or formula, if you decide to work through it more than once, you'll get something new out of it every time. It'll challenge you in different ways every time. It'll help you learn something new every time – about songwriting, about being creative and maybe even about yourself.

And as you keep growing and learning, you'll understand more about which parts are optional or can be done in a different order. So what started as a set of strict guidelines to follow might become more of a blueprint, then a scaffold, and – if you keep writing long enough – a fond memory of a charming songwriting guide that got you writing and thinking in new ways. And that's exactly how it should be.

[2] This book is not just about 'how' – it's about '*why*'.

In this book, we won't just look at how to come up with a good title. We'll also look at what makes a good title good. And we won't just talk about how to write a good bridge. We'll talk about why you would – or wouldn't – want to include a bridge in the first place.

That's because the exact songwriting process I'm about to talk you through is really only the second most important part of the book. What's most important is the way all of the different parts of the process help you understand *why* it makes sense to write a song in this way.

Because even if this process is just one process, the way all of the parts link together definitely isn't – it's based on the deep, fundamental principles of how songs work.

You can think of these principles as the 'whys' of songwriting – why a good song idea is so important, why a good title should capture your song idea, why repetition in your melody makes it catchy, why you want to start your verses with a strong or dramatic line. We'll cover all of these, and much, much more.

And honestly, that's one of the biggest advantages of approaching songwriting through a process instead of a method or a formula – you'll learn a ton of techniques and ideas that you can apply in every single song you write for years to come. (And again, that's one of the reasons you'll still get plenty out of this book, even if you aren't a beginner.)

That's also why, if you stick with it, this book will completely change the way you look at songwriting – it'll help you understand not just what to do, but why you're doing it. Then, if you build up enough experience to want to write songs in a different way, you'll be in the perfect position to do it, because you'll have a ton of fundamental, universal songwriting principles you can rely on to create something fresh, original and polished.

And sure, doing that probably makes this book longer than it would have been if I'd set out to create The Ed Bell Method®. Explaining those fundamental principles means I'm not going to hold back on the detail, and occasionally we'll have to go fairly deep into some music and songwriting theory.

But as the saying goes, "Give a man a fish and he'll eat for a day. But teach someone to write songs and they'll spend the rest of their life making a ton of really cool stuff." So all that extra detail will be worth it, I promise.

[3] This is a book about using your instincts.

One thing that doesn't get talked about enough in songwriting guides is that there's really no way to write a good song without relying on your instincts. Sure, there are tools and principles and techniques you can learn, but figuring out whether you've used them well is usually more about making an instinctive judgment than making an intellectual calculation.

Plus, if you want to write something that connects with people, you have to do that by making human judgments – you can't just calculate the perfect song by following step 7.4b or using foolproof formula #923.

That's really the biggest reason that songwriting formulas or methods aren't helpful – they usually take away the instinctive, messy, human part of songwriting and make it more like filling out a passport application.

And sure, I get it. It's scary to try riding a bike without stabilizers for the first time. It's scary to start writing a song without knowing exactly where the creative process will take you. And it's scary to trust your instincts if you're not used to trusting them.

But it's also a lot more fun. It's also a lot more rewarding. And it's also the only way to create something that's genuinely original – that captures even just a bit of who you are as an artist and a human being.

And while some people think it's better to learn the basics of songwriting and then start thinking about all of that stuff, I don't. As far as I'm concerned, it's something you might as well start doing now – as scary and as exciting as that might sound.

And if you were wondering, if you're new to songwriting, of course your creative instincts won't be as sharp as they'll be after you've got a few songs under your belt. If you're a beginner, of course you're going to find it harder to trust your intuition. But how do you think you develop those instincts in the first place? You guessed it – you practice using them. So one of the most important ways this process is different is that I'm going to give you the creative freedom to do exactly that.

And sure, giving you this much creative freedom means there might be moments in this process when you feel stuck or confused. But that's how songwriting works. That's part of the challenge of creating new things. Every new song is a leap into the unknown – so no matter how experienced you get, every songwriter feels stuck or confused sooner or later.

In other words, the difference between beginners and experienced writers isn't that experienced writers never get writer's block – it's that they've picked up tons of reliable tricks and techniques to keep themselves writing, and they've built up the determination and resilience to trust the process, trust in themselves, and keep going, confident that they'll figure everything out eventually. (Because if you keep going, you usually do.)

To help you get there, I've filled this book with tons of practical techniques and ideas to get you through the most common songwriting pitfalls and blocks. But it's also up to you to keep persevering so you can start fine-tuning your instincts and building that creative resilience that's going to pay off for literally the rest of your life – and not just in songwriting.

[4] This book is about writing the songs you want to write.

Another reason instincts are so important in songwriting is because personal tastes play a huge part in the way you answer the question 'what should a song be?'. Ultimately, whether you feel like writing a pop song, a rock song, a rap song, a country song, or something else entirely, it's mostly your instincts that tell you what a song should sound like and say. And since exploring your own personal style is a big part of songwriting, again, you might as well start developing those instincts right now.

That's why the process in this book gives you so much freedom – so you can use it to write whatever kind of song you like, based on your musical tastes and interests, and with whatever instruments or technology you have on hand.

And if you're not completely sure what your personal 'sound' or style is yet, that's totally fine. In the same way it takes practice to hone your creative instincts, it takes practice – and a lot of songs – to figure out your personal style.

So for now, the best thing you can do is just to let your tastes and interests take you where they want to go, even if, for the moment, that sounds a lot like some other writer or artist. Because the more you explore, the more you'll uncover what your personal songwriting style is.

That said, there are two specific areas in this process where you're going to follow a specific format or way of thinking that are worth mentioning.

The first is in the song's **structure** or **form** – the way the song and its sections are put together. There are a handful of different structures songs often take, but for this process, I'm going to walk you through how to write using the most common one: a **verse-chorus structure**.

That's because to make this process make sense – without making it really, really long – it has to be based around a particular structure. Also, since verse-chorus structures are so common, learning to write them is one of the most important songwriting skills you can pick up. And while there are actually a ton of different sections you can include in a verse-chorus structure, we're going to focus on the most important ones – verses, choruses, bridges, intros and outros. (If you want a quick summary of this structure before you start, you can check out Appendix 3.)

The second area is in the specific way we're going to approach writing your song. While the process in this book is really, really versatile – as you know, you can use it to write virtually any kind of song you can imagine – it follows what's sometimes called a 'melody and lyric' approach to songwriting. So after figuring out what you want to write about, we're going to start building the song by piecing together melodies, lyrics, chord progressions and instrumental grooves in a logical and organic way.

That's opposed to what's sometimes called a 'track and hook' approach, where a producer creates a beat (or track), usually without thinking about the content of the song, before someone else adds a vocal melody (or topline, or hook) and lyric.

The 'melody and lyric' approach isn't automatically better, but it's usually a better way of exploring how the different parts of a song all work together. And since that's one of the main goals of this book, it makes sense to approach songwriting that way here.

But even if those two factors affect how this book works for you, it will still give you tons of freedom to explore this process – and do all of the trying, messing up, learning and trying again that songwriting is all about – in whatever styles or genres of music you like. So make the most of that.

So there you go. That's what makes this book work, that's what makes this book different. And that's why – and how – this book is going to let you be truly creative.

And now we're getting closer and closer to the moment you'll finally get to start creating your song's music and lyrics. But before we do, there's one other important topic we should cover.

SECOND THINGS SECOND: YOU DON'T SUCK (I PROMISE)

So, this is kind of awkward. But just in case it needs to be said... just in case you need to hear it... and just in case the 'if you think you suck' part of this book's title really resonated with you... I have good news:

No, you don't suck.

At all.

I promise.

Because if there's one thing songwriting books don't talk about enough, it's this – songwriting is *hard*.

And sure, creating anything new is hard. Creating anything out of nothing is hard. But in songwriting specifically there are tons of things – rhyme, structure, melody, chords, grooves, textures, vocal range, energy levels, phrasing, stress, repetition, motif, story, style, and plenty more – you're supposed to think about all at once. So it's no wonder that songwriting sometimes feels like playing a game of five-dimensional chess, upside down in the dark, while you simultaneously try to file your taxes, learn Polish and cure cancer.

And naturally, since songwriting is so hard, sooner or later most writers get stuck or hit a wall or think 'damn, I suck at this'.

And if that's ever happened to you, I have even more good news:

It means you're normal. It means you're human.

In fact, if you've ever told yourself you suck, I actually have great news:

It means you have standards. It means you care about what you create. And most of all, it means you're a writer. (Congratulations.)

We've already looked at the myth that great songwriters are born and not made, and thrown it in the trash where it belongs. But there's another myth that belongs in the trash (or at least the recycling) as well – that being an experienced songwriter means you've got it all figured out, that you always know exactly what you're doing.

I'll level with you – I've been writing songs for more than twenty years, and I'm still not always sure what I'm doing. Despite everything I've written already, despite everything I know about songwriting – and despite writing a ton of books on how to write songs – every new project still feels like I'm starting from scratch, like I'm really just figuring it out as I go along.

Because the truth is, I kind of am starting from scratch on each new project – so I am figuring it out as I go along. Every new project is a project I've never made before, so I can't know exactly what I'm doing. I can only figure it out by trying a ton of stuff to see what works.

And sure, with experience that gets easier. And you do get faster. But you never quite reach the point where you've got it all figured out – at least, you don't if you're being ambitious and creative enough.

And so, if every new thing you write is a creative adventure to some place you've never been before, of course you're going to feel lost or stuck sometimes. That's just part of making new things.

But there's hope. There's always hope.

Because even if you think you suck at songwriting, there's a simple way to gain more writing experience and help convince yourself you actually do know enough about songwriting to get started. It's a powerful and universal law of songwriting that goes a little bit like this:

To suck less, write more.

That's it. That's the secret to success, happiness and personal fulfilment in songwriting.

You don't have to be great at songwriting to get started. But you do have to get started to become great at songwriting.

You can't wait until you feel confident to get started. You have to get started to earn that confidence in the first place.

And that means the only way to be better at songwriting in the future is to be comfortable with not being so hot at it now.

You have to be comfortable separating the ideas that while you might suck at something you haven't done much – whether that's pole vaulting or cake decorating or songwriting – you yourself, as a person, don't suck. And then you can use the motivation and self-esteem that separation gives you to go practice that thing and get better at it.

Or, in the words of actress Carrie Fisher, "Stay afraid, but do it anyway. What's important is the action. Just do it and the confidence will follow."

Or, in the words of some anonymous graffiti I once saw in Brooklyn, "Be brave enough to suck at something new."

So let's not pretend – there are parts of this process that will be hard. There are parts of this process where you'll feel like you're spending more time staring out of the window and sharpening your pencil for the seventy-eighth time than writing. And there are parts of this process where you'll think 'Wow, this song sucks' and even 'Wow, I suck'.

And again – that's normal. That's called 'the creative process'.

But it's up to you to control the narrative on that. It's up to you to remind yourself that none of those things are reasons to give up. It's up to you to keep going exactly when things get hard because, as you know, that's the only way to get better — and the only way to get a song finished.

My job in this book is to give you a roadmap for writing a song from scratch. My job is to explain every part as simply and plainly as possible without dumbing anything down. And your job is to keep going. To keep trying new things. And to remember that if, sooner or later, you think you suck, that probably means you're on exactly the right track.

So here's to the art of figuring it out as you go along. Here's to the joy of never really knowing what you're doing. Here's to the thrill of thinking you suck sometimes. *C'est la vie*, my friend — or at least, *la vie créatif*.

And here's to the art of doing what you've got to do anyway.

Because, more than anything, that's what songwriting — and life in general — is all about.

THE SONGWRITING PROCESS:
A SUMMARY

Here's a fun idea. Let's try it.

Wait. This is harder than I thought.

Damn, this new song sucks.

Damn, I suck.

Hold on. Let's just keep going...

Actually, this song is OK.

No – this song is DONE and it is GREAT.

AND FINALLY:
HOW TO GET THE MOST OUT OF
THIS BOOK

OK, we're nearly there – you're on the brink of writing the first words and notes of your song. But before we jump in at long last, we should talk about four ultra-practical ways you can get the most out of working through this process.

If you've been writing a while, some of these ideas might not be new to you – but whatever level you're at, they're worth taking seriously, as they'll make working through this book much easier and much more worthwhile.

Work Through the Parts in Order

I know. I know. I just made a huge deal about how the process in this book isn't the only way to write a song, how one of the biggest thrills of songwriting is writing in new ways, and how you're a unique snowflake in a vast universe full of infinite creative possibilities, yada, yada, yada.

But let's forget about that for now.

Because just like if you come to my gig you'll have a much better time if you don't start yelling at me from the back to change the setlist, if you follow the process I created you'll have a much better time working through this book.

As I said, I've crafted all ten parts carefully so they walk you through a logical, step-by-step process that builds neatly on the parts you've already completed. So while in real life, yes, the different parts of a song could come to you in any order, this book won't make much sense if you start working on Part 9 when you're not even halfway through Part 3.

That said, if you're writing your chorus lyric in Part 3 and you get a flash of inspiration for what you could write about in your bridge in Part 9, that's great. That happens – and it's often a blessing when it does. So any time that happens to you, the best thing you can do is to jot your idea down so you don't forget it, then come back to it when it's time to use it.

To help you out as you work through this book, I've split up the main text with a series of 'action boxes'. You'll spot them easily because they come with a lightning bolt symbol – to represent the god- or goddess-like way you're going to put this book aside and go create something amazing. I've put these boxes at the ideal points to stop reading and get creating, using the ideas we'll have just talked about. Each action box also comes with a few bullet points that summarize the main ideas worth thinking about while you write that part of your song.

So yes, if you're really keen, there's no harm in reading ahead a bit to understand what's coming next. But don't *create* ahead – do the action boxes in the exact order they appear. Even if it takes a while to work through one particular action box. Even if finishing one particular action box is hard work.

Most of the later action boxes rely on what you create in the earlier action boxes. So just stick with the program. At least for now.

Oh, and finally – as well as the action boxes I've included a few bonus 'toolboxes' in a handful of places in the book. These come with a hammer and spanner symbol to represent, I guess, the god- or goddess-like way you can learn more about a handful of advanced songwriting topics if you want to. They're completely optional, and this process will still make sense without them, but if you decide you want to go beyond the essentials and understand topics like rhyme, chord progressions and copyright in more detail, that's what the toolboxes are there for. (This book also has an index right at the back if you want to look up any of its concepts later.)

Work Through at Your Own Pace

While all of the action boxes look similar on the page, working through them will be different every time. You might finish some quickly. You might finish some more slowly.

That's completely normal. You might have had more practice at some areas of songwriting than others. Some action boxes are more complicated than others. Some days you'll be feeling more creative than others.

And again, that's just how it works.

So don't rush the process. Take it at your own pace. Give yourself the time and space you need to work through it on your own terms. Always.

Exactly how and when you decide to work through this process is completely up to you, and chances are it's going to take you weeks, not days. And if you're new to this – or you're just interested in improving your creative process – I have three suggestions for how to carve out some quality time to write:

- **Make a plan and commit** – Decide what days or what exact times of day you're going to write, then stick to it.

- **Cut out all the distractions** – Turn off your phone, unplug the Internet, tell everyone you live with to leave you alone.

- **Try to enjoy the ride** – Some days it comes more easily than others, but sometimes a slow writing session is just preparation for a really productive one next time. Embrace that.

And for those days when you really, really don't want to write – or the days it's coming slowly – literally the best thing you can do is make yourself a really simple promise: you'll try for at least 20 minutes.

That's it. 20 minutes. After that, you can take a break and go do something else. But from the moment you sit down to write, you'll do nothing other than try for 20 minutes – even if it comes super slowly, even if it doesn't come at all.

Because I promise, nine times out of ten, you'll find your flow within 20 minutes and want to keep going even longer. Sometimes it just takes that long to warm up. Just like sometimes you have to run a tap for a second to get past the stale, stagnant water, sometimes you have to get past some bad writing to get to the good stuff later.

So any time you don't feel like writing, just promise yourself you'll try for at least 20 minutes. More often than not, you'll be glad you did.

Write Solo or Co-Write if You Prefer

I designed this process so you could use it to write on your own – but if you want to co-write, or collaborate, with someone else, it absolutely works for that too.

Co-writing is a great way to learn from other songwriters, master the art of collaboration and help each other stay inspired and on track. But equally, writing solo is a great way of exploring your personal tastes and interests, taking everything at your own pace and discovering what you're capable of creating on your own.

So it's up to you whether you want to work through this book solo or with someone else – or even work through it a few times in different ways.

If you do co-write, you'll have to be extra organized about how you're going to get through the process. Will one of you focus mostly on music and one of you on lyrics? Will you collaborate in real-time together on each section? Will you split the song into sections and focus on one each? Because this process is split into parts that focus on specific song sections – and usually writing either the music or lyrics to those sections – it's completely possible to split this book up in any of these ways.

On the other hand, if you're used to co-writing and have decided to try this process completely on your own, don't worry. Because I've made this book as beginner-proof as possible, it doesn't matter if you're new to writing music or lyrics (or both). As I've said, we'll cover everything you need to know. And even if you work through this process alone but plan to keep co-writing on everything else in the future, that's great – you'll learn a lot about how entire songs work by working through this process solo at least once or twice.

Still, if you decide to co-write your way through this process, what's most important is that you agree on a definitive plan for who will create which parts of your song – and when – so you can keep moving forward.

Save All of Your Drafts

As you'll find out, one of the big ideas of this book is that it's good to try out tons of different ideas – to brainstorm, to make sketches, to think up more ideas than you can ever really use so you can pick out the best ones to put in your song.

Because that's usually the biggest difference between OK writers and great writers – it's not that great writers always have better ideas, they're just better at trying out more ideas so they can get to, and keep, only the best ones.

And the truth is, sometimes an idea that didn't seem promising at first turns out to be a great idea later – when you've thought about it, or found some other way to use it, or found out it fits perfectly in some other part of your song.

That's why one of the most important habits you can get into as a songwriter is to record as many of your ideas as you can.

Maybe that means setting your phone to record while you play around on your guitar. Maybe it means covering pages and pages with potential lyric ideas, notes and sketches. Maybe it means creating a project full of rough ideas or versions – or ending with a final project file called 'V9.2 Final Final ACTUAL FINAL (Revised)'.

I know, they make reality shows about people who can't throw anything away. They stage interventions for them. They call them hoarders. But this is different – as a songwriter you're supposed to hoard ideas. And unless you have a superhuman memory, if you don't write down your ideas, you'll probably forget them.

So if you finish this process with a three-minute song plus a pile of unused sketches, notes and ideas, that means you're doing it exactly right. (The document where I keep all the old and cut versions of chapters of this book – just in case – just hit 100,000 words. And that's a sign I'm doing something right.)

That iceberg meme everyone shares online is clichéd but it's true: your finished song is only the tip of the iceberg, and it'll sit on tons of ideas that weren't good enough, or didn't fit right, or were the OK version you had to write before you could write the great version. But it's always worth keeping track of those ideas, because you never know what you'll want to use later.

And there you go – those are the four important ways you can get the most out of this book.

All that's left to say – and I guess the fifth way to make the most of this process – is to go and have some fun. Because not only is creativity supposed to be fun, but the more fun you have while you work through this process, the more exciting things you'll create with it.

So if you're ready – at long last – to get writing, to make some creative magic, to leave your own creative dent in the universe, you know everything you need to before we jump in.

So let's do it.

HOW TO WRITE
A SONG

(EVEN IF YOU'VE NEVER
WRITTEN ONE BEFORE AND
YOU THINK YOU SUCK)

[PART 1]
FIND A GREAT
SONG IDEA

[PART 1]

FIND A GREAT SONG IDEA

In this part... | *How to choose a strong song idea – and why it's so important.*

Alrighty. We made it. It's finally time to start creating.

If you're like most songwriters, you're probably eager to dive in and start writing the words and notes that will become your song. But before you do that, you've got a really fundamental decision to make – what your song is going to be about.

One of the ideas we'll come back to again and again in this book is that, however you write a song, pretty much no songwriter starts their song at measure 1 or line 1 and just writes from there. Songs are built part by part, often by starting with the bigger picture and zooming in from there. And that's exactly why your first important step is to start thinking about your song's big idea, situation or message – what you might call the creative vision for the song.

So let's talk about how this works.

WHY A GREAT SONG IDEA MATTERS

One of the defining features in any great work of art is a sense of unity. It's the feeling that everything in a painting belongs there. It's the feeling that every part of a building serves a bigger function or purpose. It's the feeling that every scene in a movie adds up to tell one single, powerful story.

And as a songwriter, there are lots of things you can do to make a song feel unified. You can give it a chorus that keeps coming back. You can keep it in the same key throughout. You can make sure you don't switch the lead singer for their estranged half-sister two-thirds of the way through.

But the most important way to give a song a sense of unity is to base it on a single big idea or vision. It's starting a song by saying 'I want to write a song that says _____', or 'I want to write a song that's about _____', or 'I want to write a song that does _____ and _____'.

In fact, that pretty neatly encapsulates the fundamental idea of songwriting that this part of the process is all about: **a great song is based on a single idea you can summarize in a single sentence.**

You might call this your song's idea, or vision, or elevator pitch.

And making sure everything in your song is centered around one thing in this way is a really powerful strategy for at least two reasons.

One, it makes your song much easier for your audience to understand. It gives them a single focus to understand your song through. It makes sure it doesn't feel like your song's verse is about one thing, its chorus is about something else, and its bridge is about something else again. And it helps make sure that your song feels familiar quickly, because you're not asking your audience to get their heads round seven different song ideas within a single three-minute song.

And two, it makes your song much easier to write. That's because, as you'll see, once you've figured out your song's big idea, everything else in this process – your song's title, your song's chorus lyric, even the way your song sounds – is going to come from it somehow. (That's the 'why' part of this book we talked about in the introduction.)

And that's not only going to make this writing process more streamlined, it'll also take out a lot of the guesswork around what to write next or what might or might not work. Because instead of just guessing, having a big vision or idea helps you figure out what's going to fit with what you've written already so your song sounds unified and not like a patchwork of cool but unrelated ideas.

And sure, some other time you write you might start out with a cool guitar riff, or a line of a lyric, or a title, or something else. And that's fine.

But even if you do, it's usually hard to make any firm decisions about what your song's music should sound like and its lyric should say until you've found a single focus to organize the entire song around.

That's why when people say 'idea is everything' in songwriting, they mean it literally. Everything in your song is going to come from the big idea or vision you come up with in this part.

So let's start figuring out what that could be.

HOW TO PICK A GREAT SONG IDEA

So, as we talked about, your goal here is to decide on a single-sentence 'elevator pitch' for your song. It's to find that single idea or spark that's going to help you create every single word and note in the rest of your song.

And honestly, there are a few different ways of doing that, but in songwriting it usually comes down to another really fundamental idea: that **songs tell stories**.

Yes, I know – songs aren't *War and Peace*. They're not *Avatar*. They're not the *Lord of the Rings* trilogy. Most songs are based on simple, direct stories like 'I love you' or 'we're breaking up' or 'you did WHAT with my sister last summer!?'.

These are all stories because there are people involved, there are emotions involved, there's a backstory or a history or at least a situation. And even if most songs are based on simple stories, thinking about song ideas like this is a powerful way to give you tons of rich material to build a finished song out of.

That's why, for example, you don't find many songs based on the big idea 'A song about gravel'. There's nowhere to take that idea. It's not a story. There's no situation there.

But make it 'a song about a girl who's creeping down a gravel driveway at 2am to see her boyfriend while he's asleep in the house' and already there's tons to write about. Why is she creeping? How did she end up in this situation? Is her boyfriend expecting her or is he about to get a big surprise?

So what that means for you is that, as much as possible, you want to be thinking up song ideas that create a miniature world. You want to aim for song situations that are interesting and exciting to you – situations that exist in more than one dimension.

And here's the trick with this: spend some time brainstorming a few different ideas. That's right – even if you want to base your song on one single idea, the way you get there isn't just to think up one idea, declare yourself an unmatched genius and move on.

You want to come up with a few song ideas – maybe related, maybe completely different – to give yourself way more options than you need so you can pick out the one you're most excited about. (You'll want to get used to this, by the way, because you'll be doing it again and again in this book.)

So let's get brainstorming.

To keep things simple – especially if this is your first song – I recommend you stick with three common and tried-and-tested song formats:

- A 'direct address' song – where one person sings something to one specific other person. Like a love song, or a breakup song.

- A 'to the world' song – where your singer has a message to share with anyone who'll listen. Like a song that says 'I'm back', or 'Nobody's gonna stop me', or 'Racism is wrong'.

- A third-person 'story' song – where your singer is basically a narrator who tells the story of a specific person or group of people.

So have a think. See what song ideas come to you. Anything goes – whether it's based on these three formats or not. Try to come up with at least five but up to ten different ideas, and try to write them down in a single 'A song about _____' or 'A song that says _____' sentence. And try to keep things as simple as you can – the best song ideas are usually astoundingly, even painfully, simple.

As I said in the Introduction, take as much time as you need. Think about the three different formats above if you need to and see what comes to mind. (And if you're really, really stuck, skip ahead to Appendix 1 where there's a quick list of 21 song ideas you can use.)

But however you do it, go where your interest and your curiosity lead you. Focus on what's important or what matters to you right now – because if it's a song idea that you're excited about, chances are other people will be excited about it too.

BRAINSTORM SOME SONG IDEAS

- **Come up with at least five – and up to ten – potential song ideas.**

- **These can be rough at this stage, but try to focus on stories and situations that seem interesting to you.**

- **Try to condense each idea as a specific, single 'elevator pitch' sentence.**

OK. Nice work.

And now you've got a few different ideas, all that's left is to pick out your best one and flesh it out a bit before you move onto the next part.

First, you'll need to settle on a single idea.

So take a look at your list of song ideas and see what really jumps out at you. Which ideas inspire you the most? Which ideas seem most exciting to you? Which ideas make you think 'oh, a song about that sounds really cool'?

Again, the only rule is to go with the idea you're most excited about. And again, there's no need to rush. Take as much time as you need to settle on a song idea you're inspired by.

And if there are two or more ideas you feel equally inspired by, that's great. Just pick one – and maybe save the others for later. There's no right and wrong when it comes to picking a good song idea – it's only what sounds interesting to you.

And if you're not sure whether it's the 'perfect' song idea, that's fine too – because nobody ever is.

Say it with me: taking a chance on a new song idea is always a leap of faith. And honestly, half the trick in writing a good song is taking an idea and doing something bold with it.

So in short – now is a great time to trust your instincts, jump and see where they take you. Chances are, you'll pick out a great idea. But even if you don't, you'll probably end up with an OK song and even sharper instincts for next time – which is a pretty great outcome too.

Once you've settled on a single song idea, you're going to need to flesh it out a bit before you can use it. And that means figuring out answers to three important questions:

- Who is singing?

- Who are they singing to?

- What are they trying to say?

So under your single-sentence song idea, try to answer each of these questions. Maybe like this:

> **A song where the singer breaks up with his girlfriend.**
>
> **Who is singing: A mid-20s guy**
> **Who are they singing to: His girlfriend of two years**
> **What are they trying to say: I love you but it's not working for me anymore and we have to break up.**

Or like this:

> **A song that's an uplifting message to the world saying "chin up, things will get better".**
>
> **Who is singing: Me, the singer**
> **Who are they singing to: Anyone feeling down**
> **What are they trying to say: Stay positive. Things will get better.**
>
> **Maybe the singer's just been through a tough time and wants to pick everyone up a bit? She could use parts of her story to encourage other people.**

As you can see in the second example, I also included a few extra notes and ideas. Doing this is totally optional, but if anything comes to you while you're clarifying your song's big idea, it's worth getting those ideas down, especially if they help answer why your singer has to say what they have to say. Any extra ideas or background will help you when it comes to writing your lyric later.

And that's it. That's the first part done. And that's all there is to finding the great song idea that's going to see you through the rest of the process.

So spend some time picking out the song idea you want to move forward with, and make sure it's fleshed out enough to be useful in the next part. Then I'll see you there as soon as you're ready.

 CHOOSE A SONG IDEA

- **Pick out the 'elevator pitch' song idea you're most excited about working with.**

- **Underneath, write down your answers to these three key questions: 1) Who is singing? 2) Who are they singing to? and 3) What are they trying to say?**

- **If any other background details or information related to your song idea come to mind, you can jot those down too.**

[PART 2]
CHOOSE A LYRICAL HOOK (OR TITLE)

[PART 2]

CHOOSE A LYRICAL HOOK (OR TITLE)

In this part... | *How to use your song idea to pick a strong lyrical hook, or title.*

OK. Next up in this journey through time, space and songwriting, it's time to think about writing your song's **lyrical hook**, or title.

If you've been writing songs for a while, you'll probably have heard the word 'hook' already. One of your goals in writing a song is to make it as memorable or catchy as you can, and one way songwriters do that is by including plenty of 'hooks' – musical and lyrical ideas that are repetitive and distinctive enough that they hook onto your listener so they won't forget your song any time soon.

And that means pretty much anything can be a hook – a catchy vocal melody, a neat guitar riff, even a specific drum rhythm or some kind of instrumental solo.

But a song's lyrical hook – a word or phrase that's repeated a lot within the song's lyric, and is usually also the song's title – goes deeper than that. Lyrical hooks aren't just about using repetition to make your song memorable or catchy – if you choose a good one, they also help your listener understand what your song is about.

And just to clarify: yes, most songs' lyrical hooks are also their titles. So 'Yesterday' or 'I Want to Break Free' or 'Single Ladies' are all lyrical hooks that are also titles. So a lot of songwriters just call them titles. But I don't, because sometimes – for reasons I talk about in more detail in my book *The Art of Songwriting* – a song has a title that's different from its lyrical hook. So just to be clear, in this book we're going to use the term 'lyrical hook'.

In a verse-chorus song, the lyrical hook almost always goes in the chorus. We'll talk about exactly how that works in Part 3, but for now, your job is to come up with the word or phrase you're going to use as your song's lyrical hook.

And in short, that comes down to one important principle: **a good lyrical hook is a word or phrase that neatly encapsulates what the song is about.** (Remember when I said every other part of your song is going to come from your big song idea somehow?)

So 'Yesterday' is a song about how some guy's love life all started going wrong, well, yesterday. 'I Want to Break Free' is a song about someone who's trapped in a relationship they want, uh, to break free from. And 'Single Ladies' is a song with a message about loyalty and self-respect directed specifically to, you guessed it, all the single ladies.

And to do this yourself – to take your song's big idea and use it to pick a lyrical hook – here are a few important guidelines:

- Sometimes a lyrical hook is a snappy summary of the song's message – like 'I wish you'd told me' – and sometimes it's related to that message more loosely – like 'Little white lies'.

- If you're feeling adventurous, a lyrical hook can be more ambiguous or cryptic – like 'Don't hide away' – or even metaphorical – like 'Out in the cold'. (You've probably spotted how all of these different hooks are based on the same song idea, only some express it more directly than others.)

- But whatever you pick, a good lyrical hook – like any good lyric – sounds natural and conversational, like a person speaking. So 'Little white lies' is a good lyrical hook, but 'The problem of dishonesty' isn't, because nobody really speaks like that.

- Plus, a good lyrical hook is usually fairly specific. 'Don't' and 'Going on' wouldn't usually make strong lyrical hooks, because on their own they don't mean much. Your lyrical hook won't give away everything that your song is about, but it helps if you choose a word or phrase that gives us a clue. So something like 'Don't lie' or 'What's going on?' would be much better.

- Speaking of how much your lyrical hook should give away, there are no rules about how long or short it should be. But as a general rule, good lyrical hooks can be anything from a single, impactful word – like 'Lies' – to a phrase or complete sentence of maybe seven or eight words – like 'If I find out what you're hiding' or 'Tell me the truth'.

And that's basically all there is to making this short but important part of this process work.

So like in Part 1, take some time to do a new brainstorm of anything that could be a good lyrical hook for your song. And like in Part 1, anything goes – just try to think up a ton of specific words or phrases that relate to your song's big idea, or express your song's big idea, or just feel connected with your song's big idea somehow.

Try not to edit or filter yourself just yet – sometimes the best idea sounds like the craziest idea at first. And just focus on writing down at least ten different ideas – but aim for fifteen or twenty if you can – that could be a great lyrical hook for your song.

DECEPTION SONG
LYRICAL HOOK IDEAS

I wish you'd told me	Lies
Don't hide away	Lies hurt
Tell me the truth	Little white lies
Don't lie to me	Too many lies
Hidden secrets	Let me in
I can't do this	All I wanted was honesty
If I find out what you're hiding	Say it
Out in the cold	Stop hiding from me
Outside alone	Honesty is free
What's going on?	I can't with you

And once you've done that, like in Part 1, it's time to pick one to move forward with.

And like in Part 1, a lot of this comes down to instinct. All of the lyrical hooks I came up with in the bullet points would work for a song based on the idea of someone saying 'Tell me the truth', only in different ways. But depending on the kind of song you want to write – and the kind of writer you are – some of them will sound more interesting and fun to write with to you.

So take your list of lyrical hooks, and see which of them really stick out to you. Figure out which ones seem extra interesting or captivating to you. Maybe they express your song's big idea directly, maybe they're interesting because they're a more original or unusual way of expressing your song's big idea. For now, let's assume your song's title is going to be its lyrical hook – so if one of your options just sounds like a cool title word or phrase, that's great too.

Or – as sometimes happens – if looking over your list of potential lyrical hooks gives you a new great idea, go with that. Sometimes the ideal lyrical hook comes to you by combining or mixing up a couple of the ideas you already had.

But however you do it, settle on one single word or phrase that you feel encapsulates your song's idea, subject or message in a way that sounds good to you. Then write it down somewhere – on a new sheet of paper, on a post-it note, wherever you like.

Because next, it's time to start working on your song's lyric by turning your lyrical hook into a complete chorus.

CHOOSE A LYRICAL HOOK

- Take your song's central idea or message and try to think up at least ten potential lyrical hooks that encapsulate that idea or message well.
- Then pick out the lyrical hook you're most excited about from that list. Try to pick a word or phrase that's interesting and that expresses your song's idea in a conversational way.

[PART 3]
WRITE THE CHORUS LYRIC

[PART 3]

WRITE THE CHORUS LYRIC

In this part... | *How to use your song's lyrical hook to build a complete – and catchy – chorus lyric.*

OK. Now it's time to get started writing your song's actual lyric. And to do that, we'll start with the chorus.

And if you were wondering why we're going to start writing in the middle, it's because in a verse-chorus song, your chorus is usually the section that really gets to the heart of what your song is about. It often makes sense to start writing there, because once you've cracked the heart and soul of what your chorus is going to be, it usually makes it easier to build the other sections of your song around it.

That said, there's no reason we have to start writing your song lyric first. While it might make sense to start writing your song's chorus before anything else, the real answer to the age-old question 'Should you write music or lyrics first?' is 'It doesn't matter'. Plenty of great songs are written music first and plenty of others are written lyric first. And actually, plenty are written in tandem – a bit of music, a bit of lyrics, some other bit of music, some other bit of lyrics – and honestly, as long as the music and lyrics fit together in the end, what you wrote first doesn't matter.

But to keep things simple, we're going to focus on one part at a time, starting with your chorus's words. And to do that, we'll use the lyrical hook you chose in Part 2 to build a complete chorus lyric – and save writing your chorus's music for Part 4.

So, to do that I'm going to recommend you write an 8-line chorus lyric. There's no rule that says chorus lyrics have to be eight lines. And plenty of chorus lyrics aren't eight lines. But 8-line choruses are pretty much the standard in songwriting, and they're usually not too tricky to make work, so that's what I recommend you aim for.

There are basically two things you're trying to achieve when you write the lyrics for your chorus.

First, you want to incorporate your song's lyrical hook prominently within your chorus. That's because if your chorus is the section where you really get to the heart of what your song is about, and your lyrical hook is a word or phrase that helps make that clear, you want to make sure your lyrical hook is featured prominently.

In practice, that often means putting it in a prominent position – like the first or last line – and/or repeating it a few times to make sure your audience really gets that it's your lyrical hook. (Honestly, a big part of making a hook sound 'hooky' is just repeating it a lot.) So as a general rule, it's good to aim for at least two or three repetitions of your lyrical hook in an 8-line chorus.

Second, for the parts that aren't your song's lyrical hook, you want to come up with words, phrases and ideas that explore or expand on what your lyrical hook is saying. In other words, you want to blend your lyrical hook into your entire chorus lyric seamlessly, so it doesn't sound forced or shoehorned in.

We'll talk specifically about what this means for writing choruses in a second, but for now it really comes down to one important general rule: **you want every line in your song's lyric to relate back to your song's big idea somehow.**

Wow. I know. That's sounds like a wild theory. But it's true – in a good lyric, pretty much every single phrase, idea and image is related somehow to the song's overall message or idea. Nothing in the lyric is random or an accident – it all works together to explore that one big idea.

And yes, it's another example of why having a single, clear idea for your song is so important – because, like we talked about in Part 1, it gives you a focus that everything else in your song can stem from.

Let's talk about exactly how this applies to writing your chorus lyric.

PLACE YOUR LYRICAL HOOK

So if your two main goals for your chorus lyric are to feature your lyrical hook prominently, then surround that lyrical hook with words and phrases that support it somehow, there's a pretty much unlimited number of ways you can make that happen.

But in this process, let's start by thinking about where you're going to put, or place, your song's lyrical hook in your chorus, then focus on building the rest of the lyric around that.

If you're new to songwriting, I strongly recommend you place your lyrical hook in lines 1, 3 and 7 – because that's a format that works well for most lyrical hooks and isn't too tricky to work with. (And because that's the format I'm going to talk through in much more detail later.)

But if that seems over-repetitive for the lyrical hook you chose, or this isn't your first time at the rodeo and you want to mix things up a bit, you could try placing your lyrical hook just twice in lines 1 and 5, or 4 and 8 instead. (Again, there are no rules about how and where to repeat your song's lyrical hook – these are just a handful of simple but effective formats. I talk more about all of this – plus other common formats for placing your lyrical hook – in *The Art of Songwriting*.)

THREE SIMPLE HOOK PLACEMENTS IN AN 8-LINE CHORUS

1 HOOK	1 HOOK	1
2	2	2
3 HOOK	3	3
4	4	4 HOOK
5	5 HOOK	5
6	6	6
7 HOOK	7	7
8	8	8 HOOK

So to get started, I recommend you take out a pad of lined paper or open a blank document and just write or type this:

1
2
3
4

5
6
7
8

I know. It's a pre-lyrical masterpiece. And you'll probably never guess how I came up with it. But seriously – you'll get rid of these numbers later. They're just there to help you construct your lyric in the meantime.

Next, place your lyrical hook according to the format or scheme you want to try.

If your lyrical hook is a complete phrase or sentence, that's going to be pretty straightforward because your lyrical hook will fill the line. So if, say, your lyrical hook is 'I wanna dance with somebody', your chorus lyric will look something like this:

1 **I wanna dance with somebody**
2
3 **I wanna dance with somebody**
4
5
6
7 **I wanna dance with somebody**
8

If your lyrical hook is a single word or just a couple of words, you could use it on its own and end up with some very short lines – and occasionally that works well. But more likely you'll want to incorporate that hook word or words within a longer line that makes sense as a complete phrase.

So for a lyrical hook like 'Over You', you might come up with something like this:

1 I'm so over you
2
3 I'm so over you
4
5
6
7 Oh, I'm so over you
8

Or, if you want to push yourself a bit more, you could pencil in a few different ways of leading into your lyrical hook:

1 I'm so over you
2
3 I'm finally over you
4
5
6
7 You bet I'm over you
8

And if you go with this more ambitious plan, just one extra tip: while it's fine to vary how you incorporate your shorter hook however you want, you want to make sure the phrases you come up with stay equally strong – or get stronger – as your chorus progresses. (That's actually another good principle of songwriting in general: make sure what you repeat stays as strong or gets stronger as your song goes on.)

In other words, you want to be sure that the way you incorporate your lyrical hook doesn't make its meaning weaker each time – like 'I'm so over you', then 'I think I'm over you' then 'Maybe I'm over you'. That's because if it's definitely a song about being over someone, you don't want to drain the lyrical hook of its impact by using it in a more doubtful way as the song goes on.

Whatever format you choose, get your hook in as many times as your plan or format demands it. (And if you stuck with the plan of using lines 1, 3 and 7 to plant your hook, congratulations – that's more than a third of your chorus lyric written.)

Then, once you've done that, we can start building the other lyric lines around the hook lines you've just added.

WRITE THE REST OF YOUR CHORUS LYRIC

Now comes the slightly trickier but more interesting and creative part – building the rest of your chorus lyric around the repetitions of your lyrical hook.

Again, your most important goal here is to come up with words, phrases and ideas that support or expand on your song's lyrical hook. And as much as possible, you want to incorporate your lyrical hook as if it just happened to be there naturally, not like you crowbarred it in because a book about songwriting told you to.

And yes, I know – we just planted your lyrical hook in your chorus lyric a few times. But that's the deception or the artifice of the art – making all of those repetitions of your lyrical hook fit in so naturally that they don't sound like you put them there on purpose. Even if you did.

So how do you do that?

To demonstrate, let's imagine you're going to use the first lyrical hook scheme I recommended before – with your lyrical hook in lines 1, 3 and 7. And then let's imagine you're going to continue creating this knock-off version of 'I wanna dance with somebody'. (Seriously though, for now it's fine to use any lyrical hook or title you like. But in real life it's usually best to avoid copying a well-known title for your song – unless it's a short or more generic title, like 'Hello' or 'With You', and you've found a fresh angle or idea to use it with.)

Anyway, in this short Whitney Houston homage I'm using to show you how this part works, here's what we've already got for lines 1 to 4:

1 **I wanna dance with somebody**
2
3 **I wanna dance with somebody**
4

...

And so, to fill in lines 2 and 4, you want to write something that extends, continues or just relates somehow to the central idea 'I wanna dance with somebody'. (Quick side note: if you placed your lyrical hook later in your chorus, like in lines 4 and/or 8, you'll have to do the reverse – instead of making the rest of the lyric spring from your hook, you'll have to write something that leads into, or aims for, your lyrical hook.)

So 'I wanna dance with somebody, because I love to dance!' is great – it gives us a bit more background and expands on the basic idea. Or 'I wanna dance with somebody, especially the cha-cha' is also a good start – because it's another expansion, and it stays on the topic of dancing.

Something like 'I wanna dance with somebody, and what the heck is for breakfast??' isn't a good choice, though. It goes completely off-topic and feels weird, even just reading it on the page.

So with that in mind, try to come up with a line 2 that feels like an extension or continuation of your lyrical hook. Here's what I came up with:

1 I wanna dance with somebody

2 'Cos dancing's what I love to do.

3 I wanna dance with somebody

4

...

I'll be honest – it's not the most profound lyric line I've ever written. But it works – it extends and expands on the lyrical hook. It stays on topic and it gives us a bit more information around the song's central idea. And the lyrical hook isn't shoehorned in – it sits naturally among all the other lines.

Line 2 is also the same length of line 1, give or take – which will make things a lot easier later, when it comes to giving your lyric a melody. And I specifically picked a line 2 that ends with a word like 'do' so I'm not going to have a hard time trying to rhyme with it.

Speaking of rhyme, if you're new to this process – and even if you're not – I strongly recommend you use a **rhyme scheme** where you try to rhyme the last word of line 2 with the last word of line 4, and ditto with line 6 and line 8. (That's often summarized as XAXAXBXB, where the lines marked 'A' and 'B' rhyme with each other, while the lines marked 'X' don't rhyme with any of the others.)

If you've been writing for a while, you might know there are a few different types of rhyme, like **perfect rhyme** ('high' and 'lie') and **near rhyme** ('high' and 'like').

You can use either type of rhyme – or a mix of both – in this process, but if you want to know more about how rhyme works, you can check out the toolbox below. (And, as usual, there's even more about rhyme schemes and types of rhyme in *The Art of Songwriting*.)

🛠 TOOLBOX

RHYME AND RHYME SCHEMES

In short, two words rhyme when they end with the same sound but start with a different sound.

Perfect rhymes are exact matches – like 'cat' and 'mat' – while **near rhymes**, or **slant rhymes**, are near matches – like 'cat' and 'mad', or even 'met' or 'map'.

When you say words with more than one syllable, some syllables get a bit of an extra stress – like in the words 'ta-BOO' or 'MOR-ning' – and that affects the way they rhyme too.

Specifically, the stress pattern at the end of the words has to match – so you could rhyme 'ta-BOO' with 'BLUE' or 'a-DIEU' or 'mis-con-STRUE'.

But it sounds weird if you try to rhyme 'MOR-ning' with 'WING' or 'ker-CHING' because the stresses don't match. So you'd have to try something like 'AWN-ing' or 'fore-WARN-ing' instead.

Some songwriters swear by perfect rhymes and some think near rhymes are more than good enough – so it's up to you which type you use. But whatever rhymes you use, it's worth looking out for **identities**, which are pairs of words that might look and sound like they rhyme, but they don't.

Two words are identities when their final stressed syllables sound exactly the same, like 'SEEN' and 'ob-SCENE', or 'BOUT', 'a-BOUT' and 'round-a-BOUT'. And because the last stressed syllables sound identical, they end with the same sound *and* start with the same sound, so they don't fit the definition of rhyme.

If you compare a pair of true rhymes – like 'bout' and 'doubt' – with a pair of identities – like 'bout' and 'about' – you'll hear that the identities don't sound as good when you say them out loud. So it's always worth using proper rhymes instead of identities if you can.

The **rhyme scheme** in a song – or song section – is the plan for how its rhymes are organized. This usually uses a notation where 'X' shows you lines that don't rhyme, while any lines that rhyme with each other are given letters alphabetically to show they match.

So for example, XAXAXBXB means rhyming alternating lines in pairs – lines 2 and 4 rhyme, then lines 6 and 8 rhyme with different words.

XAXAXBXB is probably the most common rhyme scheme in songwriting, and that's why I recommend it for this process, but there are a few other popular alternatives:

THREE EFFECTIVE RHYME SCHEMES FOR AN 8-LINE CHORUS

XAXAXBXB	XXXAXXXA	AABBCCDD

Finally, the most common way rhyme gets used in songwriting is **end rhyme** – where the final word of each line rhymes. But sometimes you can create **internal rhymes** as well – where there are two or more rhymes within a line.

If you decided to use an XAXAXBXB rhyme scheme, that means the first piece of the puzzle is to find a pair of rhymes to end lines 2 and 4. So if you came up with a great line 2 that ends in the word 'pencil' or 'Sagittarius', now might be a good time to rethink.

But if you didn't – if you wrote a line 2 that makes sense as a continuation or expansion of line 1 *and* finishes with a word that's not going to be a nightmare to rhyme, that's great.

Then, to find a matching rhyming line for line 4 you're going to do exactly what you did for line 2, except now you have the slightly harder goal of continuing or extending your lyrical hook with a line that also happens to rhyme with what you wrote in line 2.

Sometimes – and especially if you've been writing a while – you might come up with something pretty quickly. Otherwise, a great tactic is to start by finding some appropriate rhyming words or phrases that could end your line 4. So if your line 2 ends with the word 'do', that means making a quick list of words that rhyme with 'do' that also belong in the world that the song is about.

So in this case, words like 'you' or 'too' or 'through' or 'true' are great rhymes for your shortlist. But words like 'cockatoo', 'Timbuktu' or '*merci beaucoup*' aren't so great because it'll probably be hard to use them without saying something weird or convoluted, or that isn't really related to your song's main idea. And by the way, you can always use a rhyming dictionary or a site like rhymezone.com to find rhymes – but it's still important to pick words that mean something related to your song's big idea, and not just words that happen to rhyme.

Then once you've got your shortlist, you can start playing around to find some lines that rhyme and also fit with your song idea. So with my example, they could be something like 'And I really wanna dance with you', or 'Dancing is my life, it's true' or 'I wanna dance the whole night through.'

You'll probably want to try out a few different lines – at least half a dozen, but maybe more. Then, once you've got something you like – something that both makes sense within the context of your song and rhymes – you can slot it in:

1 **I wanna dance with somebody**
2 **'Cos dancing's what I love to do.**
3 **I wanna dance with somebody,**
4 **I wanna dance the whole night through.**
5
6
7 **I wanna dance with somebody**
8

And voilà – that's more than half of your chorus lyric finished.

And if you were thinking 'Wait, but doesn't line 4 basically just say what line 3 does, only in a different way?', then yes, yes it does. This is the idea that every line in your lyric should relate back to your song's main message – and as far as chorus lyrics go, that means they usually just repeat that main message over and over again, in slightly different ways, with slightly different details or wording. And while that might feel like too much repetition while you're writing, it's exactly what makes your chorus feel like one strong, joined-up thought when people hear it.

Now let's turn to the second half of the chorus.

With the second half of your chorus lyric, I'm actually going to suggest you start with line 8. That's because, as the final line in your chorus lyric, you want to go out with a bang – or at least finish with a strong final line – so that's often a good line to write first.

Again, you'll want to brainstorm a few different lines that feel like they extend, continue or complement your lyrical hook line. Except this time, if you come up with something that feels an extra bit final, or puts a slightly different slant on your lyrical hook, that's a bonus.

After I had a play around, this is what I ended up with:

1 I wanna dance with somebody
2 'Cos dancing's what I love to do.
3 I wanna dance with somebody,
4 I wanna dance the whole night through.
5
6
7 I wanna dance with somebody
8 'Cos it's my time to shine.

And I know – that final line doesn't throw the entire lyric on its head. It won't make anyone scratch their chin and reconsider the entire meaning of the lyric that came before it. And it doesn't need to.

But it does add something extra to the idea – that dancing is about showing off or letting loose. And so if you can save something for your final line that gives us that extra something, that's a really nice touch.

Now all that's left to write are lines 5 and 6. If you place your lyrical hook in lines 1, 3 and 7, lines 5 and 6 – the only place in the lyric without the lyrical hook – is a nice opportunity to go off on a mini-tangent that's still related to your song's main message, but adds a little bit of contrast.

And like before, if you've no idea where to start, a good first step is brainstorm possible rhymes to end line 6. So in my example, because line

8 ends in shine, a good rhyme shortlist probably includes words like 'mine' or 'fine' or 'nine' or even 'divine' (but not 'bovine' or 'oil pipeline').

Oh, and watch out for **identities** – words like 'shine' and 'moonshine', that aren't really rhymes because they both end with the same '-shine' syllable. (If you skipped it, there's more about identities in the toolbox on page 34.)

And then, once again, you can take your shortlist and see where it leads you to for lines 5 and 6. You're looking for a pair of lines that are still related to your chorus's main message, but maybe deviate from it just a little bit, and definitely end with one of the rhymes you jotted down.

As usual, this is a great opportunity to try a few different ideas out – because, as usual, you won't always come up with your best idea right away. It sometimes takes three, four or even twenty different tries before you find something great. So after I did that for this song, here's what I came up with for lines 5 and 6 added into the entire lyric:

1 I wanna dance with somebody
2 'Cos dancing's what I love to do.
3 I wanna dance with somebody,
4 I wanna dance the whole night through.
5 This week had me feeling down
6 But now I'm feeling fine.
7 Yeah, I wanna dance with somebody
8 'Cos it's my time to shine.

I like this version because it gives a bit of contrast in the chorus lyric by talking about the week before and helping us understand why the person singing feels the way they do.

And that's it. That's really all there is to writing a chorus lyric that incorporates your lyrical hook in a major way, while making sure the rest of the lyric expands on and supports that hook.

Again, if it takes you a few goes to come up with some lyric lines you like, that's normal. And if it takes you a decent amount of time even to come up with options for some of the lines – especially when you're trying to write lines that do three things at once – that's normal too.

As I said in the introduction, there aren't really any foolproof methods for writing good songs. All you can do is understand what you're aiming for overall, then try different things out until you come up with a solution that works.

To keep this chapter short, I saved typing out all the different lines I tried out to put this chorus lyric together – but I'll level with you, it took me way longer to write this part than it'll have taken you to read it. So don't be discouraged if it takes you plenty of time to write your own chorus lyric.

Finally, if you decide to use a different lyrical hook scheme than the one I demonstrated – that puts the lyrical hook somewhere other than in lines 1, 3 and 7 – obviously all of the principles we talked about here still apply. You still want to make sure your lyrical hook feels blended into your lyric, and it's still a good idea to aim to create a chorus lyric that says your song's core message over and over, in slightly different ways. Though of course, the exact way you make that happen will be different.

But whatever lyrical hook format you choose, it's a good idea to choose something simple and match it with a simple rhyme scheme too. And from there all you've got to do is to keep playing round with words and phrases that are related to your song's main message until you come up with something that sounds good to you.

WRITE THE CHORUS LYRIC

- **Make space for eight lyric lines and put the lyrical hook you chose in Part 2 in at least two of those lines.**
- **Now write the rest of the chorus around your lyrical hook, trying to make sure your lyric feels like it includes your hook word or phrase naturally.**
- **Stick to a simple rhyme scheme like XAXAXBXB, and try to keep each lyric line fairly short and to the point.**

So by now you should have a complete chorus lyric for your song. And if so, bravo – that's a great start.

If you want to take a moment to make any tweaks or changes to your song, that's fine. If your lyrical hook was only a word or two, you might want to tweak the lines that include it if that makes your lyric clearer or helps it flow. Or you might have other tiny changes you want to make now you've got the entire lyric in front of you. (You might have spotted I added a cheeky 'yeah' at the beginning of line 7 in my example.)

But like before, don't agonize over this forever. What's most important is that you have a working lyric so you can move forward with this process. And don't worry if your lyric looks very simple or plain on the page – that's normal. Singing a lyric always makes it richer, so it's often better to underwrite a lyric and leave it looking even too basic on the page, because once you've added music to it, that simplicity is usually really effective.

And speaking of adding music to your lyric, that's what we're going to focus on next.

[PART 4]
WRITE THE CHORUS CHORDS, MELODY AND GROOVE

[PART 4]

WRITE THE CHORUS CHORDS, MELODY AND GROOVE

In this part... / *How to write the music – the chords, melody and groove – to go with your chorus lyric.*

Bravo – you're making great progress. And to keep that up, now you'll start writing your song's music, beginning with the music that goes with the chorus lyric you just wrote.

As we talked about in Part 3, your chorus is the section that really gets to the heart of what your song is about, so it tends to be the ideal place to start creating your song's music. More often than not, once you've figured out what your chorus is going to sound like, it's much easier to build the other sections around it.

So in this part we're going to dive headfirst into a ton of powerful songwriting and composition techniques – for crafting chord progressions, writing catchy vocal melodies, and coming up with great instrumental grooves – all through the lens of how to write a great chorus.

To do this, we're going to get pretty technical in the way we look at chords, melodies and grooves – so buckle up, because this is the most epic part of the whole process. But the good news is that all of the techniques we talk about are going to be invaluable for everything you create in the future – and not just for writing choruses.

Plus, to make this mega-part easier to work through, I've split it into four sections with their own big subheadings.

In the first, you'll make a few big-picture decisions about your song – its key, time signature and tempo. From there you'll tackle writing a chord progression, vocal melody and instrumental groove, one by one.

As always, the key to this process is to work through at your own pace, and in this part especially, it's worth going slow enough to make sure you've really understood how everything works. And while the first section of this part isn't too complicated, the other three are more substantial. So even if you managed to fly through Parts 1, 2 and 3 fairly quickly, if you want to take a break between most of the sub-sections in this part, that's definitely not a bad idea.

There are also plenty of toolbox sections in this part – and like always, they're useful but completely optional. So depending on whether you want the full-fat or diet version of this part, you can either read them or not.

But either way – and without further ado – let's get started.

[4A] CHOOSE A KEY, TIME SIGNATURE AND TEMPO

Before we jump into writing your chorus's music, there a few fundamental musical decisions you need to make about your entire song first – its **key**, its **time signature** (or **meter**) and its **tempo**.

If you already know some music theory, that'll make working through this section even easier. But if you don't, no problem – we'll start by going right back to basics.

Choose a Key

Nearly every song that's ever been written is **tonal** – which means it was written in a specific **key** (or sometimes more than one key).

In short, a key in music is a collection of specific notes that come in a kind of hierarchy – where some notes are more important than others, and some of them usually get used more often than others. And choosing a key is like choosing a specific color scheme – it gives you a world and an overall feel for your song's **harmony**, or chords.

And while there are plenty of songs that change keys – or **modulate** – at some point before they end, to keep things straightforward, let's assume your song is going to stick to one key throughout.

In songwriting, there are two main types of key you'll want to play with: **major keys** and **minor keys**.

The simplest way to summarize the difference between the two types of key is that major keys sound happy while minor keys sound sad. But the truth is a bit more nuanced than that – yes, major keys tend to sound brighter and more optimistic, but minor keys can sound anything from melancholy to moody to rich to funky to soulful to anywhere in between.

MAJOR KEYS	MINOR KEYS
Usually sound bright, heroic, cheerful, or sometimes just neutral.	Usually sound more melancholy, moody, soulful, expressive or dark.

And so – going back to the concept that everything in your song comes from your initial big idea or vision – your first decision is to figure out whether you think your song's message is best suited to a major key or a minor key.

If your song's big idea is hopeful and optimistic, you'll probably want to use a major key. If your song idea is darker or more soulful, you'll probably want to use a minor key. Or, if your song doesn't fit neatly into the category of either 'mostly happy' or 'mostly sad' – and plenty of song ideas don't – you can just pick whichever type of key you think best. (There are plenty of song ideas that could work well in either type of key.)

Next, you'll want to pick the specific key your song is going to use. And while there are some musicians who'd argue that a song in A flat major has a completely different feel to a song in G major, for now the exact key you choose doesn't matter so much. You basically want to pick a key that's not a headache to write in and that works nicely for most voice types.

So, if you're a complete beginner – or at least new to keys, chords and coming up with your own chord progressions – I recommend you pick one of these beginner-friendly keys:

FOUR BEGINNER-FRIENDLY KEYS FOR SONGWRITING

	MAJOR KEYS	MINOR KEYS
Writing for piano	C major	A minor
Writing for guitar	G major	E minor
Writing with a DAW	C major	A minor

As you'll see, depending how you're writing, some keys are going to make your life slightly easier than others.

So if you're writing with a piano or DAW, C major or A minor are probably your simplest choice, while if you're writing for guitar – or banjo or ukulele – you'll be better off writing in G major or E minor. (And if you're writing with something that's not in the table, your best bet is probably either C major or A minor.)

Of course, there are other keys too. So if you already have a good understanding of music theory and feel up to speed on keys and chords, you're welcome to choose one of the more advanced keys from the table below instead.

We'll talk through forming chord progressions – including which chords you're most likely to use in each key – in plenty of detail later. But for now, if you want a heads-up to see which chords you'll mostly use in each key – so you can stick with chords you know already – jump ahead to Appendix

2 and you'll find a series of cheatsheets that outline the main chords in each of these twelve common keys.

TWELVE COMMON KEYS IN SONGWRITING

COMMON MAJOR KEYS	COMMON MINOR KEYS
C major	A minor
D major (2 sharps)	B minor (2 sharps)
E major (4 sharps)	C minor (3 flats)
F major (1 flat)	D minor (1 flat)
G major (1 sharp)	E minor (1 sharp)
B♭ major (2 flats)	G minor (2 flats)

So pick a key that works for you and your song and make a note of it somewhere – it'll be the foundation of the chord progression you're going to write later – then let's keep going.

Choose a Time Signature

If your song's key is about choosing the world of its harmony, your song's **time signature** (or **meter**) and **tempo** are about creating a foundation to create its **rhythms** on. And rhythm is all about how long or short your song's individual notes are – what happens horizontally in time as the song goes on.

The basic division of time in a song is a single **measure**, or **bar**. Most pieces of music have a steady **beat** or **pulse** – kind of like a steady heartbeat that keeps ticking away behind all of the various rhythms happening in the foreground.

A song's **time signature**, or **meter**, determines how many beats there are in each measure. If you've ever wondered why a lot of musicians count in a piece of music by saying something like 'a 1, 2, 3, 4', that's because four is the most common number of beats per bar in virtually every genre of music. You don't often hear 'a 1, 2, 3, 4, 5' because it's pretty unusual, though not unheard of, to find music with five beats in each bar.

Every time signature is made up of two numbers. The top number tells you how many beats there are in each measure. And the bottom number tells you how long those beats last.

So if a song has four beats in each measure and those beats happen to be **quarter notes** (or **crotchets**, depending which part of the world you're in), that means its time signature is **4/4**, like this:

1   2   3   4   1   2   3   4

(Don't forget, to hear the music examples in this book, you can download the matching audio tracks at **thesongfoundry.com/how-to-tracks**. The numbers in the black tabs tell you which track goes with each example.)

As you'll hear if you listen to this example, **4/4** means there's a steady beat or pulse of four quarter notes (or crotchets) in each measure. That doesn't mean every note in your song has to be a quarter note – it just means that in every measure, the total length of all of the notes and **rests** (the gaps between notes) will last the same amount of time as four quarter notes.

4/4 is by far the most commonly used time signature in music – it's so common it's sometimes called **common time** – and it's also a really great and really versatile choice for songwriting. You can write pretty much any kind of song in any style with any message in **4/4** and chances are, it'll work well.

So unless you have a strong reason to choose otherwise, **4/4** is a great go-to choice – whether you're an absolute beginner or you've been writing for years.

Still, it's not the only choice. Another common time signature is **3/4**, with three quarter notes (or crotchets) per measure:

While **3/4** gets used a fair bit in songwriting, it's not as neutral as **4/4**. It sounds more waltz-y or dance-like, or sometimes bolder and more epic.

And finally, there are two other fairly common but slightly more advanced choices in songwriting – **12/8** and **6/8**.

These time signatures have 8s on the bottom, which means **12/8** has twelve **eighth notes** (or **quavers**) per measure, while **6/8** has six eighth notes per measure. But what complicates things slightly is that **12/8** and **6/8** are what are called **compound time signatures** – where there are really four and two main beats in each measure respectively, each divided into groups of three eighth notes.

To see what that means, compare how **12/8** and **4/4** – which both have four main beats per measure – work in this graphic:

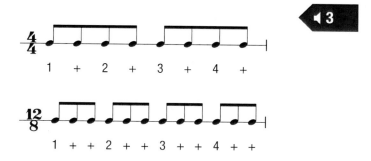

As you can see, each beat in **4/4** has one 'and' (one plus sign) after it, while in **12/8** each beat has an 'and-a' (two plus signs) before the next one. And if you listen to this example you'll hear how different they sound.

Similarly, in **6/8** there are really two main beats in each bar, divided into groups of three eighth notes (or quavers):

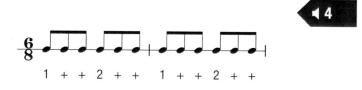

All this dividing into threes gives **12/8** and **6/8** a noticeably different feel to **4/4** and **3/4**. Both **12/8** and **6/8** tend to sound more bouncy and fun in faster tempos and more folky or 'ballad-y' in slower tempos.

So if these are your main time signature options, take a moment now to decide which one you think will best fit your song's overall vibe.

If you're new to songwriting, **4/4** is a great choice. If your song idea gives you no good reason not to go for the 'default' option, **4/4** is a great choice also. But if you want to mix things up a bit, you're welcome to try a different option instead.

TIME SIGNATURES IN SONGWRITING CHEATSHEET

4/4	The most common and usually the most versatile choice – works for virtually every style or mood.
3/4	Also a common choice – tends to create more of a dance-like or waltz-y vibe.
6/8 12/8	Common compound time signatures – both tend to create a bouncy or swung effect (in faster tempos), or a more epic or 'ballad-y' effect (in slower tempos).

Then, like before, make either a written or mental note of your choice. If you're writing in a DAW, there'll be an option somewhere on the interface to tell the DAW which time signature you want.

And from there, let's get thinking about your song's **tempo**.

Choose a Tempo

Your song's **tempo** is its speed, or the rate its beat (or pulse) ticks along. And like with your song's key and time signature, you want to make sure you pick a tempo that supports your song's overall message. A positive, uplifting song, for example, is probably going to want a faster tempo, while a sadder and more expressive ballad would probably suit a slower tempo.

And like with your key, while there are plenty of songs that change tempo somewhere in the middle, for now let's assume your song is going to stay at basically the same tempo throughout.

As you might know, tempo in music is usually measured in **bpm**, or **beats per minute**. So 60bpm – a pretty slow tempo – means each beat lasts a second, while 120bpm – a moderate or 'average' tempo – means each beat lasts half a second.

But whatever tempo you're thinking of choosing, the best way to get a feel for what a specific tempo sounds like is to try it out on a metronome – either an old-school mechanical one that clicks as its metal arm swings back and forth, or a digital one you can download on your phone or bring up somewhere in your DAW. (You can also google the word 'metronome' to bring one up in your browser.)

So get your metronome clicking and find a tempo that sounds right to you. If it helps, you could try reading the chorus lyric you wrote in Part 3 over the metronome clicks in a rough rhythm, to give you an idea of what feels like a good fit for this particular song.

Tempo decisions can be pretty subjective – what feels fast in one song might feel more moderate in another. But for a rough guide that most musicians would agree with, you can use this table:

TEMPOS IN SONGWRITING CHEATSHEET

60–80 bpm	Slow tempo
80–100 bpm	Moderately slow tempo
100–120 bpm	Moderate tempo
120–140 bpm	Moderately fast tempo
140+ bpm	Fast tempo

And once you've found a tempo that feels right for the world of the song you're trying to create, you can either jot it down somewhere or enter it into your DAW. And generally speaking, while you could give a song a tempo of

187.4bpm or 103.629bpm, it's usually best to keep things simple and pick a nice round number.

A fun side note: DAW- or more pop-orientated musicians tend to go for tempos that end in a 0 or 5, like 75bpm or 130bpm, while more classically-trained musicians often gravitate towards the traditional tempo notches you find on most mechanical metronomes, which are usually in multiples of 4 or 8, like 72bpm or 132bpm. You can use whichever system you like.

And that's the foundation of your song built. Now you can hit the ground running when it comes to writing your chorus's chord progression, vocal melody and instrumental groove.

So let's get to it.

CHOOSE A KEY, TIME SIGNATURE AND TEMPO

- **Take a moment to decide on a key (tonal center), time signature (number of beats per bar) and tempo (speed) for your entire song.**
- **You have lots of freedom in choosing a key, time signature and tempo – but try to make choices that suit the overall mood or vibe of your song.**

[4B] WRITE THE CHORUS CHORD PROGRESSION

So now that you've figured out the basic parameters of your entire song, you can start writing its chorus.

As you know, you can start writing a song pretty much anywhere – plenty of great choruses start with an instrumental groove or melodic idea, or even just a rhythm. But starting with your chorus's harmonies, or chord progression, is often a good idea because chord progressions are usually fairly straightforward to write. Plus, knowing your chord progression lets you map out your chorus measure by measure, which makes building everything on top of that much easier later.

The truth is you can use pretty much any chord in any key if you're creative and daring enough, but most of the time songwriters rely on a series of common and useful chords in whatever key they've chosen.

So we'll start by figuring out what those chords are in your chosen key. Then we'll look at how to craft those chords into a finished progression.

And to make all of that make sense, we're going to have to dive a bit deeper into how chords work – how they're formed, how they fit within your key, and how you can use a few basic principles to make building chord progressions much easier. Because just like you need a basic understanding of grammar to write sentences, understanding a few of the fundamentals of musical harmony will make coming up with original chord progressions much, much easier.

If you already have a decent understanding of music theory (or you'd rather just jump into figuring out a chord progression purely by trial and error) you're welcome to skip or skim this section.

But otherwise, it'll be a really valuable intro to how musical harmony works. And, as usual for this part, everything we cover will help you understand more about how to use chords and chord progressions in everything you write from here on in.

How Chords Work: Scales and Triads 101

So, as I said, before you get started with figuring out chord progressions, it's worth understanding some of the basic music theory behind how chords work.

First, let's talk about **scales**.

Every key comes with a scale, which is all of the individual notes that make up that key, in order. So in the key of C major, the C major scale – which contains all seven **diatonic** notes, the 'regular' notes within the key – looks like this:

We're not going to go into a ton of detail about how scales are formed, but in short, any type of scale is made out of an exact pattern of **intervals** – or gaps – between each note. That's like a scale's DNA – the code for constructing it. So with the major scale 'code' you can build major scales starting on any note you like. And though they'd sound slightly higher or lower in pitch depending on the note you start on, they'd still have the same basic sound and character of any major scale.

C major is usually the first key that gets talked about because it just happens to be made out of all the white notes on the piano. With any other major scale, you have to use some **accidentals – sharps** and **flats –** to maintain the exact pattern of intervals between the notes.

And while you can add sharps or flats in C major to use any note you want, the seven diatonic notes are usually the most important, and the ones that get used the most. (The MVPs, or most valuable pitches, if you like.)

Since you can build scales and keys on any note you like, one of the big ideas of musical harmony is that everything is relative – that chords really only make sense in the context of the other chords around them. So as well as having note names, every note in a scale gets a number called a **scale degree**, like this:

So you'll see that in C major, the note C is scale degree 1. And the note G is scale degree 5. Because everything in harmony is relative, in a different key – like D major or G major – those notes would be in different positions in the scale, so they'd be different scale degrees.

(And yes, if you were wondering, numbers with little hats is the standard shorthand for scale degrees. Also, there's no scale degree 8 because after scale degree 7 you reach the note that is scale degree 1 again, only an octave – eight diatonic notes – higher.)

And now we've covered the fundamentals of how scales work, we can start using the notes in those scales to create **chords**.

If you're being super pedantic, a chord is technically any combination of two or more notes played at once. But in most genres of music, there's one type of chord that's most important, called a **triad**.

And as you might have guessed from the 'tri-' in its name, a triad is a three-note chord – and triads happen to be three-note chords that are built in a very specific way.

To build a triad on a particular scale degree, you start with that scale degree, add the note two scale degrees above it, then add the note two scale degrees above that. In other words, you build triads out of your key's scale notes hit-one-miss-one style, like this:

C major triad

C (D) E (F) G

So to build a triad on the note C in C major, you include the note C, skip the note D, include the note E, skip the note F, and include the note G. That gives you the notes C, E and G – which together, form a **C major triad**.

And one of the things that's interesting about harmony is that the notes C, E and G can also be used individually in plenty of other chords. But when you use them together, they form a C major triad – and when you use them together in the C of C major, they're also the triad on scale degree 1.

And since by now you're probably getting quite a kick out all the terminology I'm throwing your way, let's add some more. To help explain where each note sits within the chord, they also have their own names – the **root**, the **third** and the **fifth** of the chord, like this:

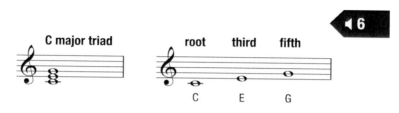

So the note C is the root of a C major chord. In a different chord it might be the third or the fifth – or not even a note in the chord at all. But these labels are important because – as you'll see later on – sometimes the chord isn't spaced out exactly like this: the root might be the lowest note, or the highest note, or a note somewhere in the middle. And it's often really useful to be able to identify which component each note is in a chord.

So now, if you apply this same idea of building triads out of scale degrees, that means you can build seven different triads on the seven diatonic notes of the major scale, like this:

And now we're really getting somewhere. If you play or listen to this example, you'll hear how there's a few different chord sounds, or 'qualities' here. Some of the chords sound brighter, and some of the chords sound darker than the others.

That's because there are three different types of triads among these seven chords. And if you count the exact intervals – or gaps – between the root, third and fifth in all of these chords, you'll spot some subtle differences.

To do that, we have to count using the smallest unit musicians usually use to measure intervals, called a **half step** or **semitone** (depending, again, on what name gets used in your part of the world). A half step is the distance between any two notes on a piano keyboard including white and black notes – or the distance from one fret on a guitar to the next one.

And so, in a C major chord, if you count the exact intervals between the notes, you'll find that the third of the chord (E) is exactly four half steps higher than the root (C), and the fifth of the chord (G) is exactly seven half steps higher than the root:

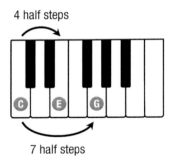

4 half steps

7 half steps

And that exact combination of intervals – four half steps and seven half steps above the root – is what makes this particular chord a **major chord**.

Meanwhile, if you do the same thing starting on the note D – scale degree 2 in a C major scale – you'll find that while the fifth of the chord (A) is still seven half steps higher than the root (D), the third (F) is only *three* half steps above the root:

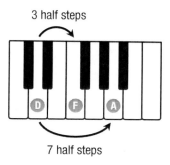

3 half steps

7 half steps

And while that difference might not seem like much, it has a big effect on the way the chord sounds. In fact, it makes the chord built on the note D using the notes of a C major scale a **minor chord**, in this case D minor.

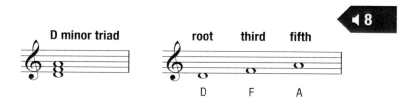

Just as major keys tend to sound brighter and more optimistic, individual major chords do too. And just as minor keys tend to sound darker and more moody, individual minor chords do too. (Though to be 100% clear, whether you write in a major or a minor key, you'll usually end up using a combination of both major and minor chords.)

And while we're on a roll with all these different terms and numbering systems, let's bring back the full set of seven diatonic chords in C major, and add even more notation. This is what's called **functional notation** – or sometimes **roman numeral notation** – and it helps explains where each chord sit within in the key, like this:

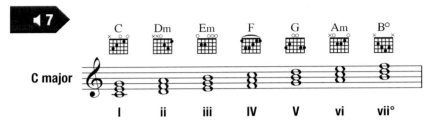

As you can see, underneath each chord there's now a number in roman numerals. Some are in capital letters, some are in lowercase, and the final chord has a '°' symbol next to it for some reason.

In a nutshell, functional notation describes the function – or purpose or role – each chord plays within the key. And because everything in musical harmony is relative – because every chord only makes sense within the context of the chords around it – this notation is really useful.

Specifically, it tells you two important things:

First, the number of the roman numeral tells you the scale degree of the chord's root. So the chord on scale degree 1 is always going to have the roman numeral I, and the chord on scale degree 4 is always going to have the roman numeral IV. (Musicians use numbers with hats for scale degrees and roman numerals for chords to differentiate between the two.)

And second, major chords are represented by uppercase letters, like 'IV' or 'V', while minor chords are represented by lowercase letters, like 'ii' or 'vi'. (And if you're curious, that '°' symbol is used to show that one chord is a **diminished chord** – which is a more unusual chord where the fifth is only six half steps above the root. But you don't need to worry about that for now.)

And so, you'll see that from building chords out of the notes of the C major scale, you get three major chords (I, IV and V), three minor chords (ii, iii and vi), and one diminished chord (vii°). (I'm sure you'll take my word for it, but you can go check the intervals within each chord if you want to.)

Now, let's quickly repeat this process in a minor key – A minor – which gives us a starting scale that looks like this:

Like C major, A minor also happens to be all of the white notes on the piano. And the reason this is a minor, not major, scale is because I made it out of the pattern of intervals for a minor scale – which is a different pattern, or a different kind of DNA, to the one that creates major scales.

And with the A minor scale, we get the same mix of three major chords, three minor chords and that one tricky (but not really relevant) diminished chord, only now they're in a different order:

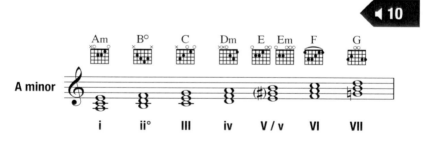

Though, as you can see, in minor keys there's an extra twist: while the chord on scale degree 5 is really chord v (a minor chord), it's much more common to **sharpen** the third of that chord – raise it by one half step – to make it chord V (a major chord). The reason for that is slightly complicated, but in short, it's because chord V is often followed by chord I (in major keys) or i (in minor keys), and that progression sounds much stronger if you use the major chord V. In songwriting, you can actually use either chord V or chord v in a minor key, but if in doubt, it's usually best to use chord V.

So that's how the seven diatonic chords are formed in each key. And now, to get us closer to being able to use the chords to build some progressions, we've got to divide them into groups of really useful chords, kind of useful chords and one chord you can mostly ignore.

To do that, let's start by identifying the three most important chords in any key, called the **primary triads**. The primary triads are chords I, IV and V in a major key, and chords i, iv and V (or v) in a minor key:

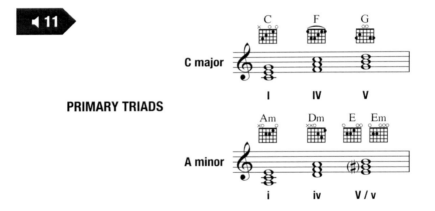

PRIMARY TRIADS

These chords are important because in most genres of music the primary triads form the foundation of musical harmony. Like the primary colors, they're not the most exciting or exotic chords, but they're the foundation of basically all musical harmony, so they're worth getting to know. (And the good news is that if you use just the primary triads, you can combine them in pretty much any order and they'll sound great.)

I go into much more detail about chord functions – about how all of the most common chords work and what you can do with them – in a big toolbox starting on page 79 if you want the full lowdown. But in short, here's how the three primary triads usually work:

Chord I or i – called the **tonic** chord – is the 'home' or 'ground' chord in a key. It's the chord you usually want to finish your song on – and often want to begin on – because it feels rested, at home and stable.

Chord V (or sometimes v) – called the **dominant** chord – is like the tonic's opposite. It sounds unsettled or unfinished – because it sounds like it wants to lead right back to the tonic. That's why chord progressions often pair up chords I and V (or i and V) to create a simple but powerful effect.

Meanwhile, chord IV or iv – called the **subdominant** chord – is a good chord to use in combination with the tonic (chord I) and dominant (chord V) as an extra color next to one or both of those chords:

67

(Like I said, you can combine the primary triads in pretty much any order and they sound great.)

Then, if you discount the diminished chord from the mix, the remaining three chords in each key are called the **secondary triads** – so that's chords ii, iii and vi in major keys, and chords III, VI and VII in minor keys:

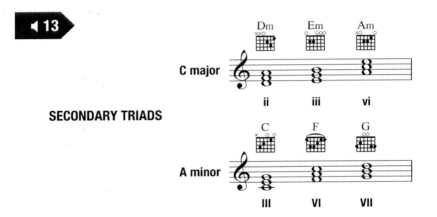

SECONDARY TRIADS

You'll notice that in major keys the primary triads are all major and the secondary triads are all minor. And in minor keys – aside from the quirk where you can use either chord V or chord v – it's the other way round: all of the primary triads are minor, and the secondary triads are all major.

There's also more about using the secondary triads in the toolbox on page 79, but in a nutshell, they're mostly used as additional chord colors – mixed with the primary triads – to give a chord progression more variety.

And just in case by now your brain is overloaded from all of the different terms and ideas I've been throwing around – we're done. That's all of the theory you'll need to make the rest of this part make sense.

So all of that covered, let's use all of the principles we've just talked about to figure out your song's chord palette within your chosen key.

Figure Out Your Chord Palette

Your song's core chord palette is the collection of chords you're going to use to write your song's chord progressions – or at least, the main chords you're going to use to do that. These aren't the only chords you could ever use in your song, but unless you have a really strong understanding of music theory, they're the go-to chords you'll want to use.

And as we talked about in the previous section, there are basically three main chords in any key you'll pretty much always want to use – the **primary triads**:

Major Key Primary Triads: I, IV, V

Minor Key Primary Triads: i, iv, V/v

Then, there are three other fun but optional chords you can use, depending on how rich you want your chord progressions to sound and how much of a challenge you feel ready for. These are the **secondary triads**:

Major Key Secondary Triads: ii, iii, vi

Minor Key Secondary Triads: III, VI, VII

And so, you know how in video games you get new tools and equipment to play with as you climb the levels? Well, songwriting isn't a video game, but if you imagine for a second it is, we can use that idea to find you a chord palette that works for you and the level of complexity you feel comfortable with.

At Level 1 – which is a great place to start if you're brand new to songwriting – you get to play with just the primary triads. That'll give you a handful of possibilities while making it virtually impossible to write a chord progression that doesn't sound good.

At Level 2 – which is a great place to start if you're fairly new to songwriting but want a bit more of a challenge – you get to play with the primary triads plus the secondary triad that usually gets used the most, chord vi or chord VI. That'll give you more possibilities, while still making it difficult to write anything that doesn't sound good.

Then at Level 3 – where we add chord ii in major keys and chord VII in minor keys – you get more harmonic options, but it'll also mean you have to work a bit harder to write something you like.

And finally at Level 4 – we add the final secondary triad to complete the set. That means you get six chords to choose from, but you'll have to work even harder to craft them into progressions that work.

Or, to summarize all of that in a single table:

COMING UP WITH CHORD PROGRESSIONS ISN'T A VIDEO GAME, BUT IF IT WAS…

	MAJOR KEYS	MINOR KEYS
LEVEL 1	I, V, IV	i, V/v, iv
LEVEL 2	I, V, IV, vi	i, V/v, iv, VI
LEVEL 3	I, V, IV, vi, ii	i, V/v, iv, VI, VII
LEVEL 4	I, V, IV, vi, ii, iii	i, V/v, iv, VI, VII, III

Instead of listing the chords in order numerically, I've put them in their rough order of importance – so you can see at a glance that in major keys, chord iii isn't normally used as much as chord IV, for example.

So now it's up to you to decide how much of a challenge you want to take on when writing your chord progressions.

The higher the level you pick, the more creative freedom it'll give you. But at the same time, with (creative) freedom comes (creative) responsibility, so at the higher levels it'll usually be harder to come up with a progression that sounds good.

Then, once you've made your choice, you'll want to translate the chord palette you chose from a bunch of roman numerals into a set of actual chords. To do that, you can either pore over all of the music theory we talked about to figure out what those chords are yourself. Or – probably a better idea – you can just use the tables on the next two pages.

You'll see I've given you a more detailed rundown of the primary and secondary chords in the four beginner-friendly keys I recommended earlier in this part, plus a quick summary table for the twelve common songwriting keys I mentioned as well.

Plus, if you want to know more about how to play these chords – whether on a keyboard or a guitar or in a DAW – at any time in this process, there's a handy reference guide in Appendix 2.

CORE CHORD PALETTES CHEATSHEET

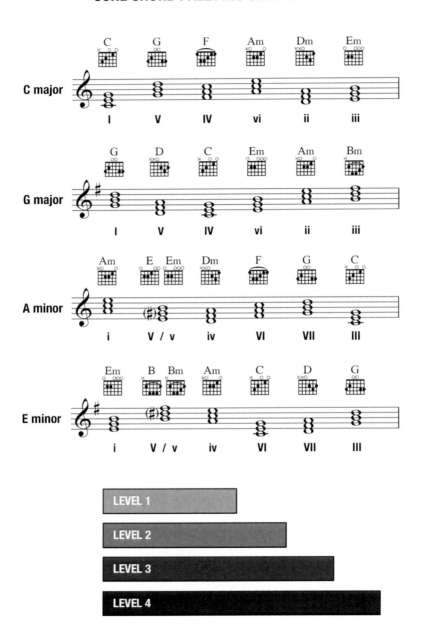

MAJOR KEYS	I	V	IV	vi	ii	iii
C major	C	G	F	Am	Dm	Em
D major	D	A	G	Bm	Em	F♯m
E major	E	B	A	C♯m	F♯m	G♯m
F major	F	C	B♭	Dm	Gm	Am
G major	G	D	C	Em	Am	Bm
B♭ major	B♭	F	E♭	Gm	Cm	Dm

LEVEL 1

LEVEL 2

LEVEL 3

LEVEL 4

MINOR KEYS	i	V / v	iv	VI	VII	III
A minor	Am	E / Em	Dm	F	G	C
B minor	Bm	F♯/F♯m	Em	G	A	D
C minor	Cm	G / Gm	Fm	A♭	B♭	E♭
D minor	Dm	A / Am	Gm	B♭	C	F
E minor	Em	B / Bm	Am	C	D	G
G minor	Gm	D / Dm	Cm	E♭	F	B♭

Write Your Chord Progression

All right, now it's the fun part: creating a progression from the chords you've given yourself to play with.

A **chord progression** is just a sequence of chords that feels – like the name suggests – like it progresses or moves somewhere. So coming up with a good progression is just about figuring out a combination of chords that sounds good to you. And, like always, no matter how much music theory you know, the only way to find out for sure what sounds good is to try a ton of different things and see what you like. (Though again, for more specific ideas about how to use each chord, there's a toolbox on page 79.)

But other than that, here are a few general principles of writing good chorus chord progressions:

- First, you'll need to decide how long your chorus is going to be overall, so you know how many measures to write chords for. And as a rule of thumb, it's a good idea to assume that each line of your lyric is going to be two measures long. That won't always be true – sometimes it'll be double or half that – but two measures per lyric line is a great starting point. So if you stuck to the 8-line lyric format I recommended in Part 3, that means you're aiming for a 16-measure chorus.

- Second, let's assume your chord progression is going to be mostly one chord per measure. That's another songwriting rule of thumb that's definitely not set in stone – plenty of songs have measures with two or more chords, or the same chord for two measures in a row. But for now, let's assume you're going to write one chord per measure.

- And third, let's assume you're going to build your chord progression out of four-measure, four-chord units. Four-chord progressions are a staple of songwriting – they're short enough for your listener to grasp easily, but long enough to be interesting, even if you end up repeating them a lot. So if in doubt, four-chord progressions are a great place to start building your song's harmonies.

With all that in mind, usually the best place to start writing your chorus's chord progression is to take the chord palette you just chose, and try combining those chords in different ways until you find some four-chord combinations that sound good and feel like a good fit for your song.

So if your song is in C major, you might have settled on the chord palette C major (I), G major (V), F major (IV) and A minor (vi). By playing around with these chords, you might discover a handful of progressions that sound good, like this one:

◀ 14

| C | F | Am | G |

And this one:

◀ 15

| C | Am | G | G |

And this one:

◀ 16

| F | C | F | G |

As usual, it's a good idea to try a few things before you settle on a final version. And as you can see, while you mostly want to move to a new chord each measure, you can absolutely use the same chord more than once in a progression, including in two measures in a row.

Then let's assume you decide that the first of these options is the one that feels like the best fit for your song. From there, the simplest way of extending this four-measure progression to fill all 16 measures of your chorus is just to repeat it four times, like this:

◀ 17

	C		F		Am		G		
	C		F		Am		G		
	C		F		Am		G		
	C		F		Am		G		

And as simple as that might look, it's a really great way of using a four-chord progression – and plenty of great choruses are built on simple repetition like this.

Still, if you want to try something a bit more adventurous, you could try to build an 8-measure progression from the chords in your chord palette, then repeat it twice to fill all 16 measures:

◀ 18

	C		F		Am		G		
	Am		Dm		F		C		
	C		F		Am		G		
	Am		Dm		F		C		

(You'll see I expanded the chord palette slightly in this example by including D minor, chord ii.)

Alternatively, there's a way to get the best of both worlds – make the most of the simple repetition of a four-chord pattern without making it feel too repetitive. One great way to do that is what's sometimes called a '1+1+2' progression. That's a format where you have a four-bar progression ('1') that repeats again exactly ('1'), then starts to repeat but gets extended into a new 8-bar unit to finish ('2', because it's twice the length):

◀ 19

	C		F		Am		G	
	C		F		Am		G	
	C		F		Am		G	
	C		Dm		F		C	

If you listen to this example, you'll hear how it sounds repetitive but not too repetitive, which is an important balance to strike in pretty much every part of a song. And this example works especially well because the changes at the end let it finish on a C major chord – chord I, the 'home' chord. That makes the chord progression sound nice and finished.

So that's the gist of using your chord palette to come up with a good chorus chord progression.

Obviously, if you're writing a four-chord progression but picked a chord palette with more than four chords, that means you won't use every one of them, and that's fine. And – as you'll see from a couple of my examples – sometimes you'll even use the same chord twice within a four-measure unit, and if it sounds good, that's fine too.

Of course, the primary and secondary triads are by no means the only chords you can use in a chord progression. So if you have a more advanced understanding of music harmony – including things like seventh chords, suspended chords, pedal points and chord inversions – you're welcome to apply what you know to your progressions here. Or, if you're working within one of the chord palettes I suggested but you chance across some other chord that sounds great, you can absolutely use that in your progression too. Though if in doubt, simple four-chord progressions work really well – so there's no need to write anything particularly advanced unless you really want to.

In fact, in general, your chorus chord progression isn't worth stressing over all that much. Yes, your chord progressions do matter. Yes, you want your chord progressions to fit the overall mood and style of your song, like everything else. But chord progressions often don't make a huge difference to the sound or vibe of a song, so it's a good idea to settle on something that works instead of spending hours and hours discovering the 'perfect' chord progression. Sure, you should experiment and play around, but once you have something that works, let's keep moving.

Again, if you need any pointers on exactly which chords you have to play with and which notes make up those chords, I've included all of that information in Appendix 2.

And finally, as I've mentioned, if you want to know more about the art and science of how each specific chord tends to work within an entire progression, there's an extra-long toolbox section over the next few pages that talks about that in a lot more detail.

WRITE THE CHORUS CHORDS

- **Use your song's key to figure out the important chords – the chord palette – you're going to use in your song.**
- **Play around with those chords until you find a progression you like. Simple four-chord progressions work great.**
- **You can either repeat that chord progression over and over to fill your song's chorus, or – if you like – repeat but vary it a little to come up with something more advanced.**

CHORD FUNCTIONS

In musical harmony, a chord's **function** is the role or effect it has within a particular key. Of course, there are tons of different ways to use each chord – but good chord progressions tend to rely on a handful of tried-and-tested chord functions, and in this toolbox we'll talk through a few of the most common ones.

Chord I or i

Chord I – or chord i in minor – is traditionally called the **tonic chord**.

As the chord in the privileged position of scale degree 1, you can think of the tonic as the 'home' or 'base' chord. That means that generally speaking, any time your song uses the tonic chord it'll feel most at rest, or at home.

That makes chord I (or i) a common choice for the beginning of a chord progression – where it feels like the home chord you take us away from – or the end of a chord progression – where it feels like the home chord you've brought us back to. It also makes the tonic the most common choice for the final chord of your song, because it makes the song sound finished.

Chord V or v

Chord V – sometimes chord v in minor – is traditionally called the **dominant chord**.

In some ways the dominant chord is the opposite or the counter to the tonic chord. Finishing a phrase on the dominant chord tends to make it sound open or unresolved, and in general, the dominant chord wants to move – or resolve – to the tonic chord.

To show you what I mean by that, let's talk about two types of **cadence** – which is a traditional term for the chords at the end of a musical phrase.

Here's what's called a **perfect cadence** or **authentic cadence** – V then I in major keys, or V then i in minor keys:

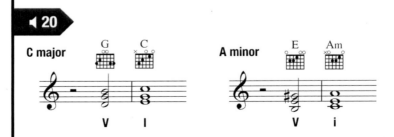

It sounds finished. It sounds final. It sounds resolved.

Compare that to an **imperfect cadence** – like these I–V and i–V progressions:

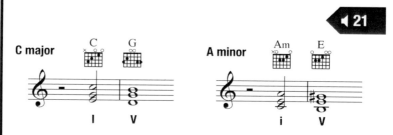

As you'll hear, it sounds unfinished. It sounds like there's more to come. It leaves us hanging. Because that's what finishing on chord V does – it makes us long for a return to the tonic chord and leaves things sounding incomplete.

For that reason, an imperfect cadence can actually be *any* chord followed by chord V, not just the tonic, and the overall effect will be the same.

That makes chord V a good choice for the final chord in your verses if your chorus starts on chord I (or i) because it'll make your verses sound unfinished or open, so they lead really nicely into the chorus that comes after them. But chord V gets used within plenty of chord progressions too.

As I said in the main text, in minor keys you can use either chord V, a major chord, or chord v, a minor chord. If you compare a V–i perfect cadence with a v–i perfect cadence, you'll hear that the V–i cadence sounds strong and final, while the v–i cadence isn't as powerful but sounds kind of funkier:

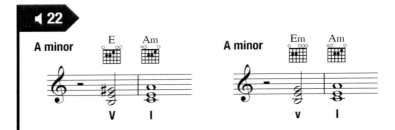

That's why chord V is usually the go-to choice in minor keys. But if you want to use chord v instead for a different effect, that can work too. But as a general rule, it's a good idea to stick to one type of dominant chord in each song – either chord V or v – and not mix and match them.

Chord IV or iv

Chord IV – or iv in minor – is traditionally known as the **subdominant chord**. And while the subdominant doesn't sound as rested as the tonic (chord I), it definitely doesn't sound as loaded or unfinished as the dominant (chord V). It usually combines nicely with both chords though, either before or after them.

The IV–V progression (or iv–V in minor) is another common type of imperfect cadence, but chord IV also has its own type of cadence with the tonic (chord I) known as a **plagal cadence**:

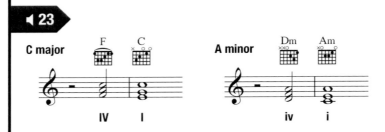

Plagal cadences can be useful in songwriting because they create the same finished and final effect as a perfect cadence. But sometimes a perfect cadence can feel too decisive or traditional, and a softer IV–I or vi–I progression sometimes sounds better.

In fact, in general, chord IV or iv is often a good 'flex' chord, either falling back onto chord I or i, or flexing away from it to come back, like in these two four-chord progressions made out of the three major primary triads:

◀ 24

| C | F | C | G | |

◀ 25

| F | C | G | G | |

Chord vi or VI

Chord vi in major and VI in minor is usually the most important of the secondary triads. It works nicely with the primary triads by adding a bit of a different color, since it's the opposite chord type (minor in major keys, and vice versa).

Chord vi or VI often work nicely in the place of chord I or i. In fact, there's one other type of cadence we should cover where chord vi or VI is commonly substituted for chord I or i, called an **interrupted cadence** or **deceptive cadence**:

◀ 26

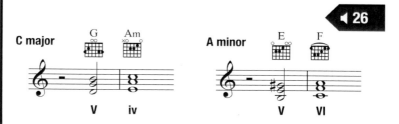

You can probably hear where the name 'interrupted' or 'deceptive' comes from – it sounds like the V chord should go to I or i, but it goes to vi or VI instead. (An interrupted cadence can also surprise us with any other chord – anything other than I or i – but chord vi or VI is usually the most common choice.)

That's the theory at least – and while cadence theory is a useful way of looking at your core chords' relationships with each other, most songwriters don't think about writing cadences specifically. It's more something they bear in mind while crafting chord progressions that fit the particular mood and vibe of their song.

Still, a four-chord progression might include a combination of the four main cadence types, like this old favorite:

| C | | G | | Am | | F | | |

Or it might start with chord I and end in chord V like a 'mega' or 'drawn-out' imperfect cadence, like this:

| C | | Am | | F | | G | | |

Chords ii and iii in major keys

There's not much to add about chords ii and iii in major keys – the four chords we've just covered are usually the most important chords you'll want to use.

That said, chord ii is often a good substitute for chord IV, especially before chord V in a ii-V progression. That's because of something called the **cycle of fifths** (or **circle of fifths**) that basically says moving from one chord to the chord five scale degrees below (or four above) tends to sound great – like from a G chord to a C chord, or from an A minor chord to a D minor chord.

We don't have space to talk about the cycle of fifths much further, but it's one reason perfect cadences are such strong progressions – they go from V to I, five scale degrees below. And if you work backwards from that, you can create the progressions ii–V–I (like Dm–G–C) or even iv–ii–V–I (like Am–Dm–G–C), where every chord's root is five scale degrees below the previous one. That makes these progressions sound extra strong:

◀ 29

| Am | Dm | G | C | |

Chord iii in major keys mostly works as a fresh or different chord color. It works well followed by chord IV (one step up) or chord vi (the next chord along in the cycle of fifths), but other combinations are possible too. Chord iii often works as a nice substitute for chord I – if there's a spot where chord I works, sometimes switching it for chord iii can work well instead.

Chords VII and III in minor keys

Chord VII works quite a bit differently from the other chords we've talked about so far. It can be a nice substitute for chord V that sounds more 'rocky' and less traditional.

So unofficially, you can think of VII–i in minor keys as an alternative perfect cadence (instead of V–i), or even the three chordsi, VI and VII as a more pop-sounding set of primary triads in a minor key. To hear what I mean, have a listen to these two four-chord progressions:

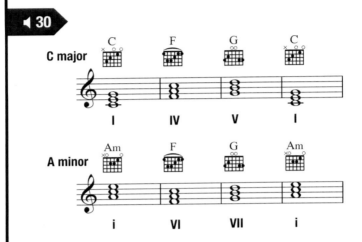

In fact, like with the real primary triads, you can combine these three chords – i, VI and VII – however you like and it'll sound good.

Chord III in minor keys works similar to chord iii in major keys – it's another chord color to try out, and often works well as a substitute for the tonic chord (chord i).

[4C] WRITE THE CHORUS MELODY

Now it's time to add a vocal melody – or topline – to your chorus. And while there's some kind of science behind what makes a chord progression work, when it comes to writing melodies, what works and what doesn't comes down a lot more to intuition.

You know when a great melody just hits you and slides right down into your soul? Well, sure, there are techniques that can help you write a melody that does that – but there's definitely no magic formula. Instead, the best you can do is to try and write something that touches your emotions – that sounds and feels good to you – and then, chances are, it'll touch other people's emotions too.

So in the rest of this section, we'll look at a few of those techniques. But at the same time, one of the most important things you can do is to aspire to the level of savagery of classical composer Claude Debussy when he said "There is no theory. You only have to listen. Pleasure is the law."

And with that in mind, let's get cracking.

Make a Rhythmic Sketch

One of the challenges of writing a good melody – especially when you're trying to write a melody that fits a specific lyric and chord progression you've already written – is that it can feel like you're trying to think about seventeen different things at once.

So before you get into the actual melodic writing, a great first step is to sketch out, even roughly, the rhythm that your vocal melody could use.

Is it the single magic secret to great melodic writing?

Nope.

Will it take all of the trial and error out of writing a good melody?

Nope.

Is it even a technique you have to use in every single song that you write, like, ever?

Nope. Not necessarily.

But here's the thing — it is a really useful strategy for making the melodic writing process easier, whether you're a beginner songwriter or not. As you get more experienced, you'll be able to do a lot of this stage of the process on autopilot and won't need to make it its own separate step. But for now, if you're new to songwriting, it's a technique worth doing to help you focus on a few important fundamentals. And even if you're more experienced, it's a technique worth trying at least a couple of times so you can have it up your sleeve any time you might need it — because sooner or later you probably will.

So, melodies basically exist in two dimensions — a melody's rhythm is what happens horizontally, in time, while a melody's pitches, or notes, are what happens vertically, up and down the scale. This technique is about focusing on just one of those dimensions for now, to give you your best shot at creating something that sounds great when it comes to the messy trial-and-error part of building a complete melody.

And — as you'll see — starting with your melody's rhythm also helps make sure what you write will fit well with the lyric you wrote in Part 3. It'll help you build a foundation that works so you can focus on the creative side of melodic writing later.

Let's start with some rhythm fundamentals.

The first thing to think about is the way your melody's rhythm fit with the words in your lyric. In fact, it's not really about the individual words but about their syllables, the single 'sound units' that make up words when you say or sing them, and the way they fit the notes of the melody.

In songwriting, each syllable in a lyric needs at least one melodic note to go with it. So 'cat' needs at least one note. 'Llama' needs at least two. And 'screaming hairy armadillo' needs at least eight. (Yep, it's a real animal. Look it up.)

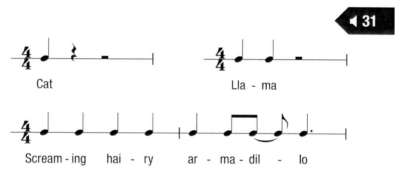

And in most genres of songwriting, one note per syllable is pretty much the default. So unless you have a good reason not to, giving each syllable one note is a great tactic.

Still, that's only one option. I said 'at least' one note per syllable because it's also possible to spread a syllable out over a few melodic notes in what's called a **melisma** or a **vocal run**.

So with a word like 'hello', you could set it as 'hel-lo', but you could also set it as 'he-el-lo', or 'hel-lo-o', or 'he-e-el-lo'. Or even — maybe if you're writing for Mariah Carey – you could write something like 'he-e-e-e-e-e-e-e-e-e-el-lo-o-o-o-o-o-ooooo':

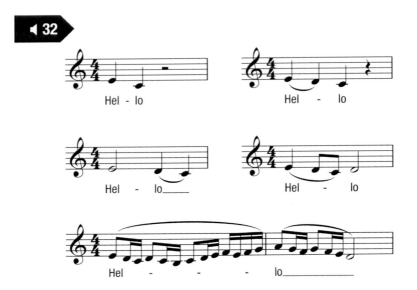

As you'll hear when you listen to this example, setting the word 'hello' in different ways creates a slightly different effect. (With some words, you even have some flexibility on the number of syllables the word has, like 'every' – which officially has three syllables, but when most people say it they usually say 'ev'ry', with just two.)

But writing a good melody – even just the rhythm – is about much more than just fitting syllables to rhythms. And part of this comes down to **prosody** – the art of combining a melody and lyric into a seamless whole.

In a nutshell, prosody is all about writing melodies that deliver the words of their lyric in a convincing and natural way.

That doesn't mean there's a single 'right' way to set a lyric to music, but it does mean that most words and phrases come with a natural rhythm and often a kind of melodic rise and fall, or contour, when you say them. (If you want to hear what I mean, try saying this paragraph out loud.)

Good prosody is about working with both of those things – or at least, not against them. So in this section you want to focus on writing a rhythm that feels like a good representation of the way you'd say the lyric in real life – not just on writing a rhythm that has the right number of syllables.

If you want to know more about prosody, there's a toolbox below that goes into more detail. (There's also even more in *The Art of Songwriting*.) But if you don't want to worry about that for now, that's fine too – just skip ahead and let's keep going.

✄ TOOLBOX

GOOD PROSODY

Prosody is the art of writing a melody that fits your lyric like a dream, or vice versa. Chances are, you want your lyric to be heard and understood, so good prosody is about combining a melody and lyric in a way that makes that as easy as possible.

And as far as rhythm is concerned, there are basically two important things worth thinking about.

Keep the Rhythm Natural, More or Less

As I said before, there's no single 'right' rhythm to give a lyric – only a handful of ways that fit and stay faithful, more or less, to the way you'd say those words in real life.

That means you want to make sure you don't write any rhythms that massively distort the natural rhythm of the words when you say them, especially by creating any weird pauses or breaks. So if your lyric contained the phrase 'I wandered lonely as a cloud', it'd sound strange if you gave it this rhythm:

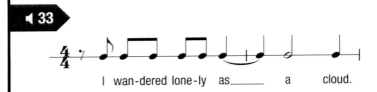

I wan-dered lone-ly as_____ a cloud.

That's because this rhythm puts really long pauses on the two words with the least meaning and emotional impact – 'as' and 'a' – which isn't what you'd do in normal speech at all. So it sounds strange. It feels distorted.

But instead, if you gave those words a rhythm like this, it sounds much better:

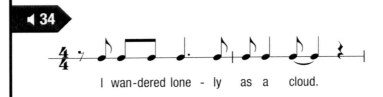

I wan-dered lone - ly as a cloud.

Again, this isn't the only possible rhythm you could give this phrase – and you might go for something a bit more creative and unusual. But you'll hear how extending the words 'lonely' and 'cloud' works really nicely because they're probably the two most meaningful words in the line.

Watch the Word Stresses

We touched on word stress in the toolbox about rhyme in Part 3, and stresses are really important for prosody too.

In short, you want to make sure the natural stresses in your lyric mostly land on the main beats within your time signature.

That's because when you say any phrase of your lyric, some of the syllables get a bit more weight than the others. So you say 'WAN-der', not 'wan-DER'. You say 'I WAN-dered LONE-ly AS a CLOUD', because if you said 'I wan-DERED lone-LY as A cloud' people would look at you funny.

And in songwriting, you want to match those stresses with the beats – you don't want to, as the saying goes, put the em-PHA-sis on the wrong syl-LAB-le.

So with 'I wandered lonely as a cloud' – which has a regular 'off-on' stress pattern – you'd want to write something like this:

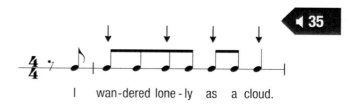

You'll see – and hear – all of the stresses land on the beats, which I've marked out with arrows for good measure. (And that first incomplete measure, if you were wondering – the one with only one beat in it – is called a **pickup** or **anacrusis**. They're really common in songwriting, and useful any time you need to put a syllable or two of the lyric before the main **downbeat**, the first beat of the bar.)

On the other hand, this is the kind of prosody that won't help you make friends at parties:

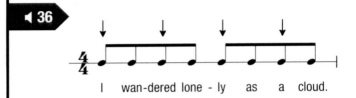

Now the stressed syllables never fall on the beats, so it sounds like something's wrong. It just makes the listener think about the weird way the words are attached to the rhythm and not, you know, the meaning of the words themselves. And that, in short, is why good prosody is so important.

With prosody, there are usually a handful of great ways to match a lyric to a rhythm — and songwriters often use plenty of creative license to make their melodies much richer or grander than normal speech. And that's great. But what you definitely don't want to do is write something that distorts or twists the natural way you'd speak your lyric to the point it sounds weird.

And for all of the theory and specifics I've just given you, as usual the best way to figure out whether what you've written works or not is to listen. More often than not, by thinking just a bit about how the rhythms you use fit the words you've written, you'll start to spot bad prosody really easily, and then you can get to work coming up with something better.

So bearing the principles of good prosody in mind, let's talk about how to start sketching out your melody's rhythm.

First of all, I recommend you think about your rhythm in **phrases**.

A musical phrase is pretty much like a phrase in speech – it's a musical statement that feels like a complete, self-contained unit. And more often than not, the musical phrases in a song are going to match the phrases in your lyric – which are usually the individual lines in your lyric.

So that means when it comes to sketching out your chorus melody's rhythm, it's a good idea to do it line by line – either in order, or at least by writing an entire lyric line at a time.

Second of all, you'll make things easier for yourself – and make your final melody easier to listen to – if you take advantage of opportunities to use repetition in your rhythmic sketch.

In Part 3, we talked about how using repetition of your song's lyrical hook helps make your song's lyric more memorable and easier to understand. Well, the same idea applies to rhythmic repetition – if you repeat the same kinds of rhythmic ideas, that'll make your final vocal melody extra catchy and more fun to listen to.

What's more, even if you give two completely different lyric lines the same or a similar rhythm, we'll still hear the rhythmic similarity between them. So rhythmic repetition is a way to make your melody even catchier than you could with words alone. (Cool, huh?)

A good way to get started on your rhythmic sketch is to set a metronome ticking or a beat looping at the tempo you decided to use earlier, and then speak the first line or one of your chorus's lyrical hook lines out loud to the beat. As usual, you'll want to try a few different things to see what you like – while you try to write something that follows the principles of good prosody, a rhythm that feels like a good match for those words.

From there, you can start to build in phrases, maybe as continuations or responses (question and answer style) to that line, like this:

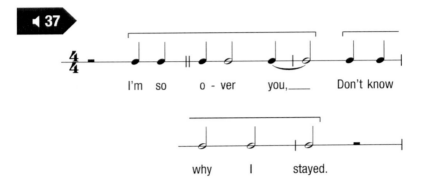

These phrases are quite short — yours might have more syllables in them — but if you play or listen to this example you'll hear how the two phrases fit together really neatly as a pair. I've marked out each phrase with a bracket above to help show you how that works.

(Both of these phrases also begin with a two-note **pickup** or **anacrusis** — two lead-in notes before the **downbeat**, beat 1, in the measure. But because each phrase contains two downbeats that essentially makes them two measures long.)

You'll also notice that each phrase finishes with a longer note, which is a good idea for two reasons. One, it creates a kind of musical punctuation to mark the end of each line, since we can't hear any actual punctuation in the lyric. And two, it gives the singer plenty of opportunities to breathe. Depending on your lyric, you might not have space to put a long note at the end of every line, but if you don't give your singer chance to breathe every two to four lines, you can probably imagine how they'll feel about that.

So those are the basics of building rhythmic phrases. But sometimes, depending on your lyric, you can take things a bit further. Sometimes you can make a few of your phrases more than just loosely responses to each other, and exact – or nearly exact repetitions – instead. Like this:

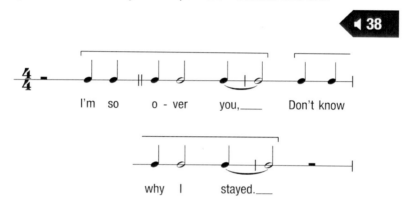

If you listen, you'll hear how both phrases have exactly the same rhythm. And while you might think that would sound boring, the exact repetition actually sounds really great. The changing lyric keeps things interesting, while the regular rhythm helps both phrases feel like they belong together. That's why it's always worth looking for opportunities to include rhythmic repetition in any melody you write – they help make your melody more catchy and memorable.

And as you get more experienced, you'll start to find more subtle ways of including rhythmic repetition within and between phrases.

To show you what I mean, here's a slightly different version of the lyric with a new rhythm:

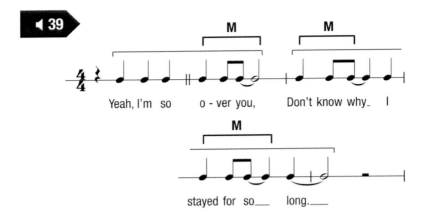

The individual components that make up a melody or rhythm are called **motifs** – they're like the individual Lego bricks you stick together to build complete phrases. (Except motifs don't hurt as much if you accidentally step on one.) In this example, I've labelled the main rhythmic motif 'M' – for 'motif', or 'magnificent', or 'maravilloso', whichever you prefer – and you'll see how it keeps cropping up. It's used in a slightly different phrase each time, but as you'll hear, all that repetition of the same rhythmic idea has a really nice effect.

(If you're really paying attention, you might have spotted this version has one main downbeat in the first phrase and three in the second, which in theory is a bit weird, I guess. But it sounds OK, so it's all good.)

I've written these examples out in notation, because that's what you do when you write a book about songwriting. But you can either work out your own rhythms by writing them down, or just by figuring them out live then recording a finished version in a voicenote or as a 'dummy' or 'guide' track in your DAW. Either way, again it's a good idea to set a metronome ticking or a beat looping while you figure out a rhythm that fits your lyric, and then you can find a way to write down or record your finished version.

I worked out my examples by following the general rule that each line of a lyric often maps neatly onto two measures of music. But if yours don't do that so easily, don't panic. That happens, even for experienced writers.

If all of your lines feel too short or long, you might be able solve everything by doubling or halving the number of measures per line – trying to fit each lyric line onto four measures or one measure.

But if that doesn't work, you might have to do some tweaking to make your lyric fit – adding the odd syllable, or taking some syllables away without changing the basic meaning of your lyric. (This seems to happen most at the start or ends of lines, where you often have to add or take away syllables to help the lines flow together.)

I know, that might not sound ideal but, like any marriage, getting your words and music to work together well takes work. And even as an experienced writer, you never really know whether your lyric is going to fit the number of measures you thought it would until you try to join them together. So stick at it and make as many fixes as you need so that your lyric fits. And if in doubt, prioritize making your lyric's rhythm make sense even if that means the lyric looks weird on the page.

So give it a go and try to come up with a decent rhythmic sketch for your chorus lyric. With rhythm especially, it's common for what you write to evolve, bit by bit, as you spot new areas you want to tweak or fix. So let that process happen – and, as you know already, let your instincts guide you towards what sounds good.

Other than that, you can let the principles of prosody, thinking in phrases, and including plenty of repetition guide you. Then once you're done, you'll have a great foundation for your final vocal melody, and you'll be ready to move on and start writing some pitches.

MAKE A RHYTHMIC SKETCH

- **A good first step in writing a vocal melody – especially if you're new to songwriting – is to focus on sketching out its rhythm.**
- **One great way to do that is to set a metronome or beat playing and try improvising specific rhythms for your chorus lyric.**
- **Try to create a rhythm that stays true to the way you'd speak your lyric in real life – or at least, doesn't distort it. And look out for opportunities to repeat the same rhythmic ideas, or motifs, in your rhythmic sketch.**

Write Your Chorus Vocal Melody

All right, it's time. You've laid the groundwork and now it's the glorious moment you turn everything you've created so far into a complete vocal melody.

That means the goal of this section is to bring together the rhythmic sketch you just created and the chord progression you wrote earlier and, with a bit of creative ingenuity, to use them to write a finished vocal melody.

And as usual, there's no secret quick fix to make that happen – there's only trying out a bunch of stuff until you find something that works.

First things first, if you've been wondering how to write a melody that fits a specific chord progression, there are really two answers. The first – as always – is that if you try out a particular note above a chord and it sounds good, then it is good. And the second – which will help you do that even more quickly – is that the notes that sound strongest are usually the notes that make up that chord.

In other words, if the first chord of your melody is C major, that means your vocal melody is probably going to focus on one or more of the notes C, E and G. Then if the chord changes to G major in the next measure, your melody is going to spend a measure or so focusing on one or more of the notes G, B and D.

So for a really simple melody, you could take the rhythm you just wrote, apply it to one note of each chord, and voilà, that's one kind of melody:

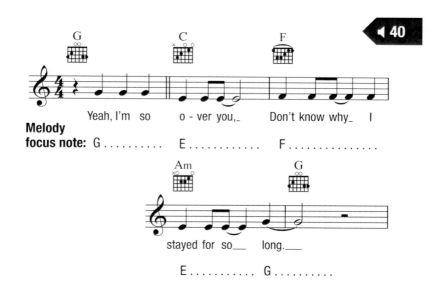

And you know what? It actually sounds pretty good. All I did was combine the rhythmic sketch I made for this lyric with the notes G, E, F, E and G to fit the chord progression.

If you were wondering where that first G chord comes from, it's because the melody begins with a pickup measure – with those three pickup notes. That means the chorus really starts on the first main downbeat – on the 'o-' of 'over' – and the measure before is really the last measure of the verse before it. For this example, I assumed the verse chord progression ended on a G chord – like our chorus progression. Don't worry about this too much, but as a general rule, you want to sync your chorus melody's first main downbeat with your chorus's first chord.

Also, if you're really eagle-eyed you might have also spotted that in the fourth measure, the G on 'long' really belongs to the G major chord in the next measure (the note G isn't in an A minor chord), though it comes a beat early. That's called a rhythmic **anticipation**, or **push**, and it's a neat melodic trick that gets used a lot in songwriting. (There are actually a handful of different ways to include non-chordal notes – notes outside of the chord – when you write. If you're interested to know more about them, there's a toolbox on page 115.)

So if you have literally no idea where to start with a vocal melody, a great first step is to pick out one note of each chord and build your melody entirely out of those 'focus' notes. (And don't knock repetitive one-note melodies, by the way – songwriters like Taylor Swift have done some pretty amazing things with them.)

But of course, sometimes you'll want to go a step or two further – especially in your chorus melody, where it's a good idea to write a melody that's bolder and makes a bit of a statement.

And just like with your chorus melody's rhythm, with full melodies one of the best ways to write them is to let them evolve. If you want to write something a bit more adventurous, sometimes you have to start by writing a really basic melody then polishing and improving it until it does what you want it to. So you might keep playing your chord progression over and over as simple held chords, or looping it in your DAW, while you play or sing slightly different versions of your melody over the top. That can take a bit of time, but it's a great way of letting your melody evolve, bit by bit, into something that really shines.

Other than that, everything we spoke about with repetition and motifs applies to melody writing too. In fact, with melodies, there's often even more room to do this – because even if you don't repeat the exact melodic motif, but you keep its overall melodic 'shape' intact, we'll still hear the connection.

You can even use melodic motifs in **inversion** – upside down – and the repetition will still help to make your melody catchy and memorable.

Here's what I mean:

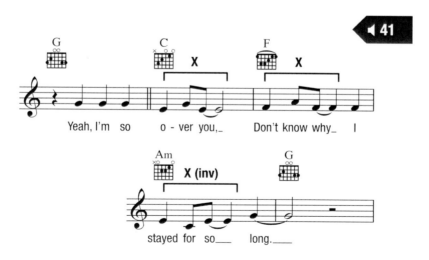

In this example, the melody keeps the same focus note in each measure like before – though this time there are plenty of other notes involved too, which makes the melody more interesting.

I've labeled the main melodic motif 'X' – for 'X-ceptional' or 'X-celsior' – and you'll see how it gets used three times in quick succession. The motif is basically a mini 'swoop' that starts out as an E–G–E melodic figure. Then I use it up a note, F–A–F, to fit the next chord – and because it's the same melodic shape, or contour, it's still recognizable as the motif. And then – my biggest boss move of all – I use the motif in inversion as E–C–E, marked 'X (inv)', and because the shape stays intact we still hear it as the motif.

And sure, I'm showing off. I went hard on repeating the same melodic motif to prove a point, and not every melody is going to repeat the same melodic motif or motifs measure after measure like this. But you get the idea: if you can look out for opportunities to repeat the same or similar melodic ideas in your chorus melody, that'll help make your melody sound coherent – like it's all one thing – as well as making it extra catchy. Because, as you know, that's what repetition does.

Like in your rhythmic sketch, it usually helps to think of melodies in phrases. So for one great way to write a complete melody – and the way I wrote the example above – try these three steps:

- Write a complete melodic phrase for the first line – or even the first two lines – of your chorus. Write whatever sounds good.

- Then, pick out one of the motifs in it – try to pick something that sounds distinctive, that we'll recognize when you repeat it. (Some songs even use an entire melodic phrase as a motif.)

- Then, focus on building the rest of the melody, phrase by phrase, trying to include that motif as much as you can.

You don't need to overthink this – melody writing isn't just some big puzzle where you have to cram the same melodic motifs in over and over. But if you aim to use plenty of repetition and let your instincts help you decide what sounds good, you can't go wrong.

Like everything else, melodies can take plenty of trial and error to get right. So don't panic if it doesn't come out perfectly first time. Revising and rewriting are just part of the process of writing good songs – and often you have to write the bad version (or versions) of something before you can write the good version.

Oh, and one extra thing: try to keep your melody's **range** – the distance from its lowest to highest note – within about an octave, say from one G to the next G above it. That'll make sure most singers can sing what you've written. (There's more on vocal range – and a few other bonus melody writing tips – in the toolbox on the next page.)

And that's basically it – keep thinking in complete melodic phrases, keep letting your instincts guide you, and keep trying new things to find out what works and what doesn't.

It's always a good idea to practice singing your vocal melody as you write it – even if you're not really a singer – to help you figure out what you like and what you don't. And of course, if you want to make any changes to your rhythmic sketch when you turn it into a finished melody, go for it. (That's why it's called a sketch and not 'a rhythm forever set in stone'.)

Once your melody is complete, make sure you record it – either by writing it down, or singing or playing it in a voicenote or track in your DAW.

Then as soon as you're ready, all that's left to add to finish your song's chorus is its accompaniment or instrumental groove. So that's what we'll look at next.

WRITE THE CHORUS MELODY

- Use the rhythm you sketched earlier to craft a complete vocal melody. Try to focus your melody around one or more notes in the chord underneath it.

- Try to think in complete musical phrases – or lyric lines – and look out for opportunities to use melodic repetition to help keep your melody unified and memorable.

- Let your melody evolve by tweaking and improving it, bit by bit. One of the best ways to do that is to try singing it out loud and letting your instincts guide you towards what sounds good.

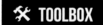 **TOOLBOX**

EXTRA MELODY WRITING TIPS

Keep Your Song's Vocal Range Within About an Octave

Try to keep your vocal melody's **range** – the span between the highest and lowest notes it uses – within roughly eight to ten notes of the scale, or an octave plus a bit. That's because, unless you're writing for a specific singer whose range you know, an octave and a bit is generally a safe range to write in to make sure most singers can perform what you've written. And while eight to ten notes might not sound like a lot to play with, it's usually more than enough. (Most songwriters stick to that range and manage to write melodies that are catchy and interesting.)

End on the Tonic Note to Sound Finished

Earlier, we talked about how ending your song on your key's tonic chord – the 'home' chord – helps make the song sound finished. And ending your chorus's vocal melody on the tonic *note* – scale degree 1 – is a great way of making it sound finished.

For the same reason, it's often a good idea to start your chorus melody on a note other than the tonic, so the whole melody basically becomes a big journey home, from there to the tonic note.

Let Your Chorus Melody Make a Bit of a Statement

We touched on this earlier, but one extra thing to think about with chorus melodies is to try to make them especially declamatory or showy – to make them sound like a statement.

That's because, again, your chorus is the section of your song that really hammers your song's idea home, so if you can, try to make your chorus vocal melody feel substantial, like it's delivering an important message. (Because it probably is.)

[4D] WRITE THE CHORUS GROOVE

So that's your chorus's music almost completely finished. All that's left to add is its instrumental or non-vocal parts.

There are lots of ways to describe a song's non-vocal parts – its accompaniment, its track, its backing – but as far as songwriting is concerned, it's worth thinking about these parts in terms of **grooves**.

In songwriting, a groove is an instrumental idea or pattern that supports your song's vocal melody and gives the song – or one of its sections – a specific character. And the beauty of coming up with a good groove is that you can get some good mileage out of it – more often than not, the non-vocal parts of an entire song section are made up of a single short groove idea that repeats and repeats, over the changing chords.

So, for example, you might come up with a groove idea that's just a specific one-measure rhythm. Then, by playing or strumming that rhythm on a C chord, then a G chord, then an A minor chord, then an F chord – all for one measure each – you could use that groove to fill an entire chorus.

That way, even though the chord the groove uses keeps changing, all that repetition helps make the overall feel and mood of the section stay the same – which helps make the section feel unified musically, like it's a single, defined song section.

We'll get to some of the techniques and ideas you can use to make that happen soon. But first let's talk more about how grooves work.

What Grooves Do

On one level, the job of your song's grooves is to accompany and support the vocal melody – or any other type of melody – on top. But great grooves don't just support their vocal lines, they enhance them, they make them richer. Or, in the words of lyricist Yip Harburg – "Words make you think a thought. Music makes you feel a feeling. A song makes you feel a thought."

That means your biggest goal in coming up with grooves is to **write grooves that capture the central mood or emotion of your song.**

We've already looked at this idea briefly when we talked about choosing a key, time signature and tempo for your song. But now that it comes to writing your song's grooves, you have a lot more opportunity to capture what your song is about through its music. And with music, you can do that in a way that we're not always conscious of – you can write something that bypasses your listener's thinking brain and slides right down into their soul.

In other words, to paraphrase Yip Harburg, your song's grooves are there to make your audience *feel* something.

And as usual, that means you want the way your song sounds to come from your song's big idea. So while you might choose a specific type of groove for a song with an optimistic message, you'd choose a completely different type of groove for a song with a sad message, or an angry message or a regretful message.

I call this idea songwriting's Holy Trinity – that in a good song, you want your song's idea, lyrical hook and grooves all to work together. Just like you want your lyrical hook to capture your song's big idea in a succinct word or phrase, you want your song's grooves to express your song's big idea emotionally through the vibe or mood they create.

SONG IDEA

LYRICAL HOOK (TITLE)

GROOVE STYLE / MOOD

And in a good song, all three parts of the Holy Trinity – idea, hook, and groove – are going to work together to create a single result or effect.

So that's the theory. Now let's see what it means in practice when it comes to writing a chorus groove for your song.

Write Your Chorus's Groove

Because your song's chorus is the central or core section of your song, you usually want your chorus's groove to capture your song's overall mood or emotion more clearly than anywhere else in your song.

The first step in doing this is to figure out the basic unit of your chorus groove. To create a sense of unity in your song, you'll want to create a short groove 'unit' of maybe just one or two measures – that you can then repeat over your chorus's changing chord sequence.

It's usually simplest if you start to write new grooves over a single chord. So if, for example, your chorus's first chord is C major, it's a good idea to build grooves that mostly use the notes C, E and G. That means one of the simplest grooves you could come up with is this:

Simply

And actually, this isn't all that bad. It works. It takes the notes of a C major chord and builds them into a one-measure unit we could easily repeat over a few different chords. It's not super busy or intense, so it won't overpower your singer's voice or distract us from your song's lyrics.

But it's not the greatest groove of all time, either. It's not particularly interesting, and – like we talked about – it doesn't give off much character. So unless you're writing a song called 'Beige, Beige, Wonderful Beige', it's a good idea to aim for something a bit more interesting and specific to the vibe or mood you want to capture in your song.

For example, if your song is a moving ballad, you could try writing something like this:

Tenderly

Sure, it's still pretty simple – and repeated or broken (split-up) chords work *great* as grooves – but this groove idea has much more character than the first one. It's starting to say something. It's starting to make us *feel* something.

But maybe your song isn't an emotional ballad. Maybe it's an upbeat song that needs a driving rock groove to help bring out the meaning in its lyric, like this:

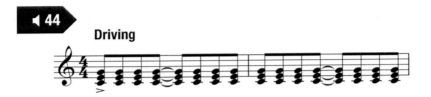

Or maybe your song would work better with a more playful, bouncy groove, like this:

Again, all I've done with these three groove ideas is come up with a few simple instrumental ideas that outlines a C major chord – using the notes C, E and G – but that would help your song capture a specific mood or character.

Of course, if you're a more experienced writer, you might want to try writing grooves that are even more advanced.

For example, here's a more developed ballad-style groove, that also starts to incorporate some non-chordal notes:

Steadily

I won't go into too much detail about non-chordal notes right now, but if you want know more about how they work, there's another toolbox on page 115. (And if you're new to reading scores like this, by the way, the two lines or **staves** are for the two hands at the piano. You can tell they should be played simultaneously because both staves' bar lines connect, plus the swirly 'bracket' on the left shows they belong to one instrument.)

But whatever kinds of groove you write, what's most important is that you write something that sounds good to you, and that sounds like it captures the overall feel or vibe you want for your song. You can write grooves in any style, using any instrument or combination of instruments, and anywhere from super simple to more detailed or complex. But that said – as I hinted at earlier – simple grooves that don't take too much attention away from your main vocal melody tend to work really well.

So here you go – this is your invitation to play around with whatever instruments or technology you have to write with, in whatever style you like, to try and come up with a few different grooves that could work in your song's chorus.

Yep, that's right – as usual, it's worth brainstorming a few different groove ideas so you can pick out the best option for your song. And sometimes – like we talked about with melody writing – good groove ideas evolve or grow out of a handful of different variations or ideas. Sometimes you realize the perfect groove is a hybrid or mashup of two or more of the ideas you brainstormed. That's another reason why it's worth trying out a few different ideas before you settle on one.

Oh, and also, if you're drawing blanks or feel really struck for groove ideas, there's nothing wrong with turning to the songs you love for inspiration. You're always entitled to be inspired by other people's songs that have a similar message or similar vibe to the song you're trying to create. Sometimes those songs will give you a blueprint for how to create a specific feel or sound through music – and as long as you copy the overall effect and not the exact grooves note by note, it's fair game.

However you do it, spend some time now brainstorming a few different groove ideas. And once you've got some options, pick out the one you think fits this song best. Then your next step is to figure out how to repeat and develop it to fill your entire chorus.

CREATE A CHORUS GROOVE

- **Brainstorm a few one- or two-measure instrumental ideas that capture the overall mood or emotion of your song.**
- **Start by building that groove idea out of the notes in the first chord in your chorus chord progression.**
- **If you're feeling short of ideas, try taking some inspiration from existing grooves you love – only make sure you transform them enough to create something original.**

⚒ TOOLBOX

NON-CHORDAL NOTES

The simplest way to make a groove or melody fit a chord is to focus it around the individual notes of that chord. And so you find a lot of grooves and melodies pretty much always using these chordal notes.

But it's also possible to use other notes – **non-chordal notes** – in your grooves to make them more interesting. As always, the ultimate way to judge which notes sound good or not is by listening to what you've written, but there are a few common and effective techniques for writing non-chordal notes which we'll talk about now.

And to do that, here's my final groove idea again, except this time I've labelled all of the non-chordal notes – everything that isn't a C, E or G – in a way that might look a bit weird at first but will make perfect sense once I've explained everything:

Even if the three notes I've labelled look kind of similar at first glance, they work in subtly different ways.

Passing Notes

The first type of non-chordal note, labelled 'P', is a **passing note**. Passing notes, as their name suggests, pass from one chordal note to another. So in this case, the passing note is an F that connects the G and E of the C major chord. Passing notes can be either ascending (part of a rising scale) or descending (part of a falling scale), and they'll sound great either way.

Leaning Notes

The second type of non-chordal note, labelled 'L', is a **leaning note**. Leaning notes are non-chordal notes that rise or fall to a chordal note immediately next door – so in this case, a non-chordal note D that rises to the chordal note E.

You can think of leaning notes as passing notes where the chordal note before is missing – so they 'lean' onto the chordal note that comes after them. Like passing notes, leaning notes can either rise or fall to land on a chordal note.

Auxiliary Notes (Neighbor Notes)

The final type of non-chordal note, labelled 'A' in the example, is called an **auxiliary note** or a **neighbor note**. You can write auxiliary notes by starting on any chordal note, moving up or down to the next non-chordal note, then returning right back to the chordal note you started on. So in this case, the note F is an auxiliary note because it's right in the middle of two E chordal notes. That makes auxiliary notes kind of like a quick 'wobble' that decorates a chordal note.

Expanding Out Your Chorus's Groove

Now you've settled on a groove for your song's chorus, that's actually the biggest creative decision in this section made. All that's left to do is to get all of that good mileage I promised out of that groove by expanding it out to fill your entire chorus, over the chord progression you've already written.

As I said earlier, the beauty of writing good grooves is that you don't need to write brand new music for every measure of each song section. You can just use the core musical idea you came up with and repeat it to fill out a section and give it a uniform feel. You're trying to 'make the most out of the least' – to take a small idea but use it to fill an entire section.

And the trick to doing that is the same idea that made all that repetition in your chorus melody effective – you can repeat a musical idea on different notes, or even alter it slightly, but as long as the musical idea's rhythm and overall shape stay more or less the same, it'll still sound like the original idea.

So to see how this idea works in practice, let's take the gentle ballad groove I came up with earlier:

Tenderly

◀ 43

(For now, let's assume this is a piano or keyboard groove – but you could easily write something similar for guitar or any other instrument.)

Next, let's combine this groove with this four-chord progression I came up with earlier:

◀ 14

| C | F | Am | G | |

That gives us four measures like this:

◀ 47

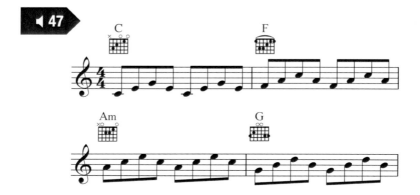

Take a moment to play or listen to these four measures. You'll hear right away what's going on – the basic broken chord groove in the first measure repeats over and over, except when the chord changes the groove moves to the notes of the new chord. And in this case, I've kept the root, third and fifth of each chord in exactly the same place each time – so the basic groove pattern is 'root–third–fifth–third' twice in every measure.

And even though it's a really simple pattern, it sounds pretty great.

But wait. We can do better.

That's because when it comes to expanding out your song's grooves – or transforming any melodic idea in a song – you don't actually have to repeat your basic groove idea exactly the same way every time. It's enough just to repeat the essence or shape of it.

To see what I mean, try playing or listening to this version:

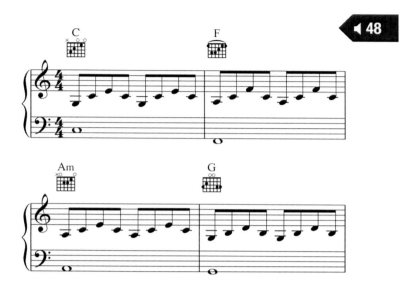

You'll probably agree that this version sounds better, or at least more consistent. And there are two main reasons for that.

First, I've re-jigged the order of the notes in some of the chords in the main groove (now in the piano's right hand, the upper staff in the score). The same chordal notes are there each time, only sometimes they're stacked slightly differently to stop the right hand jumping around so much and to keep the notes in a similar **register** – the same 'area' of notes within all the possible notes an instrument can play. This tends to make the groove sound smoother overall.

Second, I've fleshed the groove out a bit by adding a solid **bass note** (the lowest note) in the piano's left hand, the lower staff in the score. (This could also be a note in a bass guitar track in a DAW, or on a real-life bass guitar.) This gives each chord a bit of a stronger foundation – as you'll probably hear. But it also means that even though I rearranged the order of most of the chord notes in the right-hand (upper) part, it makes sure the root note of each chord – in this case the notes C, G, A and F – is still the lowest note each time.

That's important because putting a different note in the bass creates an **inverted chord** – a chord with a note other than the root at the bottom – which sounds different to a **root position chord** where the root is the lowest note. (Though inverted chords can also be useful where they're intended – usually as a way to make the song more interesting.)

So in short, while the exact notes used by the expanded-out groove might change measure by measure, the overall effect or feel of the groove stays the same. The basic pattern of the groove – its rhythm and shape – just keeps ticking away, so it doesn't matter that the notes involved are spaced out slightly differently for each chord.

That means, in summary, the expanded-out groove does this:

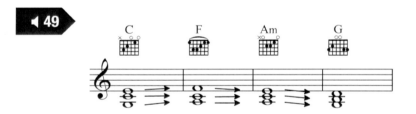

You'll see I've added little arrows that show how the exact notes the groove uses change as it passes over the four different chords. And what's neat about this example is that every time the groove moves to a new chord, each of the three notes either sticks on the same note or moves to a note nearby.

This is called good **voice leading** – as if each of the three notes in the chords is an individual 'voice' in a three-part choir – and it's the main reason the way we expanded this groove out over four measures doesn't sound jumpy and random. It sounds unified, it sounds contained and – even if I say so myself – it sounds pretty good. So that's worth bearing in mind while you expand your groove out to fill all of the measures of your chorus.

And when it comes to writing grooves in general – and especially grooves that spread out across an instrument or track's range a lot – you have a lot of freedom in how you can 'space' or 'voice' those chords.

Or, in other words, if you want to write a groove over a C major chord, you can stack the C, E and G of that chord pretty much however you like. But as long as the notes involved at any one time are either a C, E or G, it'll still sound like a C major chord. Like in all these examples:

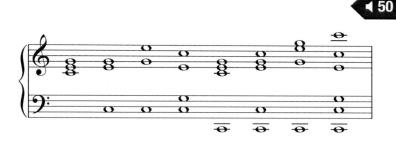

Again, if you're new to score reading, the top **staff** (or **stave**) is for the piano's right hand – the higher notes – and the bottom staff for the piano's left hand – the lower notes. And the notes that are aligned vertically are played simultaneously.

As you'll hear, the way the chords are spaced – sometimes close together, sometimes further apart, sometimes using some pretty high or low notes, and sometimes more in the center of the piano – gives each chord a slightly different effect. But because the lowest note is always C, that keeps the chord in root position and makes the chord have the same harmonic function or effect.

Some of these chords even duplicate one or more of the notes in the C major chord – and as a general rule, you want to duplicate the root and/or fifth of the chord, and not the third – but they still all sound like C major chords, because the notes they contain are always C, E or G.

Of course, you'll often want to keep your grooves spaced as closely and simply possible. But you also have the option to spread them out when it sounds good, or sounds right for the musical world of your song.

So that's the basic idea behind mapping out your chorus's groove to fill out your chorus. And honestly, with a lot of grooves, that kind of simple repetition – spread out over your entire chorus – works perfectly.

But sometimes – especially as you get more experienced – you'll want to make a few small changes to your groove's basic pattern so that your chorus isn't made up of exact repetitions of the same idea.

At the very least, you might want to tweak things at the very end of your chorus so it sounds more finished, like this:

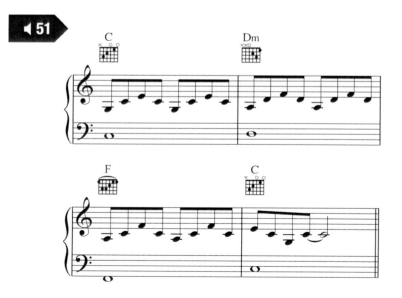

This works nicely because while the regular eighth-note (quaver) broken chord pattern does a nice job of keeping the chorus's momentum going during the chorus, finishing on a random eighth note doesn't give your chorus much of a sense of conclusion. So you might want to tweak it a little bit, like in the example above.

Equally, you might decide to tweak or develop your chorus's basic groove even more to keep it interesting. This usually means keeping the basic repeating pattern but making small changes to add a bit of extra interest, maybe like this:

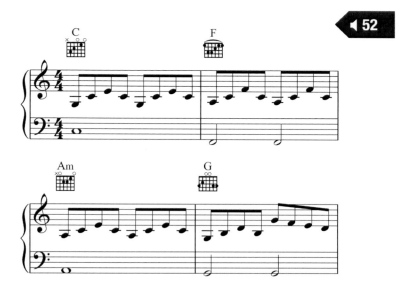

Again, this is totally optional, but as you can hear, even breaking away from the basic pattern in a really simple way in the fourth measure – and mixing things up a little in the bass part, the piano's left hand – adds some extra interest and stops the groove from feeling too repetitive.

We've really only scratched the surface of what's possible with groove writing. So if you've been writing a while, you might want to be much more ambitious in both the grooves you come up with, and how you repeat and develop them to fill your song sections. And that's great. But equally, if you're new to a lot of the ideas in this section, focusing on writing simple grooves and repeating them identically, more or less, to fill an entire section is a great approach too.

So over to you. That's how expanding out your chorus's groove works, so go spend some time figuring out what that means for you and your song.

This can be slow, technical work sometimes – especially if you're still getting your head around how chords, chord progressions, and grooves work. So stick with it, focus on repeating your groove in a way that keeps the same mood or vibe going, and you'll have it all figured out soon enough.

 EXPAND OUT YOUR GROOVE

- Take your chosen groove and expand its basic one- or two-measure unit out over your chord progression – repeat its rhythm and shape over the different chords.
- If you need to re-voice – reorder the exact notes – of each new chord, you can do that.
- After that, if you want to make any changes to improve the way your groove repeats you can – but try to maintain the feel or mood of your original groove all the way through.

And whew, that's it – for this part, at least. But give yourself a small round of applause, because that's the three main elements of your chorus's music – chords, vocal melody and groove – written, and this especially epic part of this process done.

And what's more, we went pretty far into a ton of essential songwriting techniques that you'll be able to use in the rest of this process and in everything you write in future – and that's a big deal too.

Before you continue, there's one valuable habit that's worth getting into at the end of this and all the later parts: you'll want to spend a moment to record or notate everything you just wrote, all together in one place, before moving on.

In a DAW, that's going to mean creating a project file that has your groove and vocal melody in it as different tracks. (A rough demo track of you singing or just an instrumental part playing your vocal melody works great.) If you're writing acoustically on piano or guitar and you have the skills, it's a good idea to notate what you created – either using regular musical notation or some other shorthand that's going to remind you what you wrote. (We'll look at a few different ways of doing that in Part 7). Alternatively, you could just record everything you wrote in a single voice recording, if that's a better option for you.

Again, it doesn't matter if you don't sing well, or if what you write down is rough. What's important is that you have a version of everything you created so far in one place so you don't forget it.

Once you've done that, you're definitely entitled to a breather. Then, when you're ready to continue, in Part 5 we'll start work on your song's verses.

[PART 5]
WRITE THE VERSE CHORDS AND GROOVE

[PART 5]

WRITE THE VERSE CHORDS AND GROOVE

In this part... / *How to write the music – the chords and groove – of your song's verses.*

OK. That's your chorus written, which means a decent percentage of your song – as well as the cornerstone section of your song – is done. So great work.

And after an especially epic Part 4, we're back to shorter and simpler parts – and the good news is that in this part you'll be using plenty of the ideas and techniques you already picked up as we start to think about writing your song's verses.

But before we do that, let's quickly put things into perspective, as far as your song's structure goes.

As I said in the introduction, this process focuses on building a 'standard' or archetypal verse-chorus structure. The two main sections in this structure are verses and choruses, and they're going to work in pairs

– the chorus as the big recurring section of your song, and the verses to set up and lead into the choruses. Then, after two verse-chorus 'cycles', we'll cut to a bridge to break that regular pattern before coming back home to a final chorus.

That means the main body of your song will be structured like this:

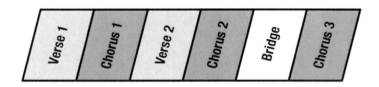

(And again, there's a more detailed summary of your song's structure in Appendix 3 at the end of the book – including a quick rundown of how long I suggest you make each section – if you want to check it out at any time during this process.)

We'll get round to thinking about your song's bridge later – as well as adding an intro and outro to frame the main body of your song. But first we're going to focus on writing your song's verses, starting with their chords and groove.

And yes, starting with your verses' music means we're going to create your verses in a different order to the way you wrote your chorus. One reason for that is just to mix things up a bit. But another is that since – as you probably know – your verses will have the same music but a fresh lyric each time, it makes sense to figure out the part that all your verses will have in common first.

So let's jump in.

WRITE THE VERSE CHORDS

First up, we'll focus on writing your verse chord progression. You could start somewhere else, but like with your chorus in Part 4, starting with a chord progression helps give you an outline for the entire section, measure by measure, so you can add everything else within that later.

For starters, I recommend you write 16-measure, 8-line verses. As a general rule, most songs have verses and choruses that are the same length, give or take. And while there are exceptions, it's generally rare to find songs that have verses that are much longer or shorter than their choruses. So however many measures and lines you gave your chorus, it's good to match that exactly in your verses if you can.

And from there, coming up with your song's verse chord progression is pretty much exactly the same process as the one you used to create your chorus's chord progression in Part 4.

Now, before we get started, you might be wondering whether you even need a fresh chord progression for your verses at all. Don't some songs just repeat the same chord progression all the way through? And the answer is yes, some do – especially songs written in the past decade or so.

And sure, I get it. YouTube and TikTok have made sure no one has an attention span anymore, so maybe it doesn't matter.

But seriously – and whether the Internet has destroyed our ability to concentrate or not – some songs work great with the same chord progression repeated throughout. Sometimes it's just a stylistic choice – what most songs do in that genre – and sometimes, if a song's lyrics, melodies and grooves are interesting and varied enough, it's fine to keep the song's chord progressions really simple.

That said, unless you really object, I'm going to recommend you come up with a fresh progression for your verses – or at least something similar to your chorus's progression but just different enough to be its own thing.

That's because – to me at least – the chord progression that goes with each section is one important way you distinguish each song section from the others, to keep your structure clear and your song interesting. So my view is that giving each section a chord progression that's at least slightly different to all the others is nearly always worth it.

To do that, you'll want to pull up your song's core chord palette again. There are songs that change keys – or **modulate** – between their verses and choruses, but since it's much more common to keep your song in the same key throughout, let's assume you're going to stick with essentially the same chord palette here. (Though if you used my levels system in Part 4 to help you figure out your core chord palette, you could use a palette up or down a level if you're up for a different challenge this time.)

Other than that, it's time to get your hands dirty again and start using those chords to come up with a great-sounding verse chord progression.

To do that, there are a few specific tactics you can use:

- If you really like your chord progression from your chorus, you could try using it with one or two small changes in your verse. So for example, the C–F–Am–G chord progression I came up with before could become Am–F–Am–G, or C–Em–Am–G, or even C–Am–F–G.

- But whatever your write, it's a good idea to base your verse around a simple repeating four-chord progression again. And like we talked about in Part 4, you could build another

'1+1+2' format and change the chord progression in the final four measures.

- If you're writing a fresh progression, you generally want your choruses to sound the boldest and most exciting, so sometimes coming up with a simpler or more toned-down progression in your verses can give your song a really effective contrast.

- Chord V, the **dominant**, is often a really great choice for the last chord of your chorus, because it's an effective 'lead-in' or 'anticipation' chord. That's especially true if your chorus's first chord is chord I (or chord i in minor key), but it usually works even if your chorus starts on some other chord. (I talk about why in the toolbox on chord functions back in Part 4, starting on page 79.)

Other than that – and we'll talk about this in more detail when we talk about verse grooves next – try to come up with a progression that feels like it's from the same musical world as your chorus's progression.

As much as it's important to create some contrast between your verses and choruses – to make them sound like different sections – one idea that we'll keep talking about is that you don't want to make them so different that they sound like they come from different songs. Honestly, using the same or a similar chord palette in both sections usually makes that happen automatically. But it's worth thinking about all the same.

So all that covered, go ahead and try a few different verse chord progressions and see what you like the sound of.

WRITE THE VERSE CHORDS

- **Figure out a chord progression for your verses. You could keep the same chord progression as your chorus, but it's good to vary it even just a little bit.**
- **Stick with the same (or a similar) chord palette as you used in your song's chorus to make sure both chord progressions sound like they're from the same world.**
- **Think about ending your verse with a chord like chord V, to help build anticipation for the chorus that comes after.**

WRITE YOUR VERSE GROOVE

Now it's time to breathe some life into your verses with their own groove. And everything we spoke about in Part 4 about grooves applies here too.

So again, the goal is to come up with a 1- or 2-measure instrumental idea that's going to sit underneath your verse vocal melody. And like before, your verse grooves don't have to be super complicated or intricate – they just have to feel like a good fit for your song's overall message or vibe.

Like with your verse's chord progression, you want your verse groove to be different to your chorus groove, but you want them both to sound like they come from the same musical world.

I know – since they're different sections you might think it's better to wow us with something that sounds completely different. But most of the time, what's most important is that your song feels like it's one thing – like everything in it belongs there – so with your grooves especially, you want to make sure everything sounds like it gels.

One great way to do that is to take one feature of your chorus's groove – maybe a rhythm, a specific melodic shape, or just the general vibe – and write a new groove idea that uses it in some way:

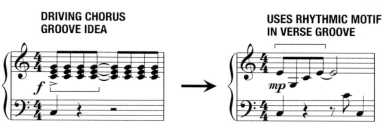

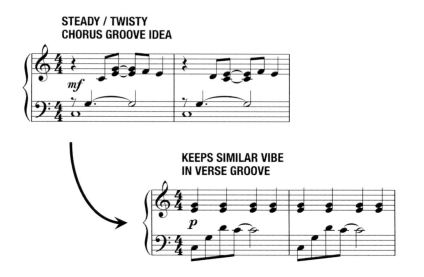

(Again, I built these grooves on the notes of a C major chord and wrote them out for piano, but you could build them on any chord or write something similar for guitar or any other instrument.)

This isn't the only way to approach writing verse grooves – and as long as you come up with a verse groove that sounds like it's from the same overall world as the chorus groove you've already written, it's all good.

Still, one extra thing to bear in mind is that verse grooves tend to be simpler or less showy than chorus grooves – like in both of the examples I just gave you. We'll go into more detail about that in Part 7, when we'll figure out how you can make your verses build up into your choruses. But for now what'll help you do that is to keep your verse groove fairly minimal, at least at first, so you can make it grow as it goes on.

If you want to see how that works in practice, the best thing you can do is to go listen to a couple of your favorite songs. You'll start to notice how simple a lot of verse grooves are at first – sometimes just simple, quiet chords, or maybe a simple rhythmic guitar idea, or maybe some held chords and off-beat finger clicks. They save something, or hold something back, so the song has somewhere to go.

Like before, it's worth trying a few different verse groove ideas so you can pick out one that really works. And also like before, sometimes you'll take the best parts of a few different groove ideas and combine them into a verse groove you really love – so take your time and keep exploring.

And then, since you'll be a pro at this by now, once you've settled on a verse groove you can go straight to expanding it over the chord progression you just wrote. (Check back with Part 4 if you want any reminders for how that works.) Then just like that, that'll be your verse's non-vocal parts completed.

WRITE THE VERSE GROOVE

- Come up with a fresh 1- or 2-measure groove for your song's verses. It's a good idea to write something new, but something that sounds like it belongs within the same musical world as your chorus's groove.
- Most verses grow in intensity and energy as they approach the chorus, so start your verse groove small and subtle – give it room to grow.
- Like you did in your chorus, expand out or repeat your groove idea over your verse's chord progression.

[PART 6]

CREATE A VERSE MASTERPLAN AND WRITE THE FIRST VERSE LYRIC

[PART 6]

CREATE A VERSE MASTERPLAN AND WRITE THE FIRST VERSE LYRIC

In this part... | *How to write your first verse lyric – and plan out your verses to make writing them easier.*

Next we'll put your verses' music to one side – we'll finish them by adding a vocal melody in the next part – and start thinking about your verses' lyrics.

As I said in Part 5, a song's verses usually all have the same chords, vocal melody and grooves – maybe with some small variations – but have a new lyric each time. That's because while the job of your chorus is to be something familiar that keeps coming back, your verses help to explain your song's situation further, and move its concept or story forward.

In this part we'll look at some powerful techniques and strategies for writing verse lyrics, but – like we've done a lot in this process – before you write even a single word, there's some important groundwork to do first.

CREATE A VERSE MASTERPLAN

If you've been writing songs a while, you might have heard about something called 'second verse curse'.

If you haven't, yes, you can tell it's something songwriters came up with because a) it's about how hard songwriting is, and b) it rhymes. And no, it's not a really weird pitch for a *Pitch Perfect* meets *The Mummy* movie, it's when songwriters write a great first verse lyric but then have no idea how to follow it up with a second. And it's pretty common.

But there's good news. No, they're not rebooting *The Mummy* franchise with a *Pitch Perfect* mashup. And no, you don't have to suffer from second verse curse – because there's a really simple way to avoid it altogether. All it takes is a little forward planning.

The way I recommend you do this is with something I call a **verse masterplan** – a big plan for giving each of your verses a specific focus or theme.

In Part 3, we talked about how a chorus lyric usually just repeats the song's main message or idea over and over in different ways. Well, your verse lyrics won't do that, but you still want them to talk about something related to your song's big idea – to set the scene of your song, add background information about your song's situation, and lead us to your song's main message in the chorus.

Again, that's the principle that every line of your song's lyric should relate back to its big idea somehow. And it's yet another way of making things easier for your audience, by giving them a lyric that's clear and focused. And it makes things easier for you by giving yourself a way to make all of the different parts of your song come from its central idea or message.

That means the trick to writing a good verse masterplan for your song is to come up with a couple of different angles or subtopics that you can focus each verse around. And in doing that, you want each angle or subtopic to be different enough to make each verse distinctive, but still linked to your song's main idea somehow. (Because, as usual, you want everything in your song to come from its big, central idea.)

It's pretty much the same idea as in essay writing. If you wanted to write an essay that argues that, say, every weekend should start on a Thursday, in each paragraph or section you'd focus on one reason that supports your idea. In one section you'd explain how a three-day weekend helps the leisure and entertainment industries. In the next you might bring up the benefits to everyone's mental health. Then in a third section you might discuss the studies that found a shorter working week also makes everyone more productive. So all of the sections would explore, support, or expand the essay's overall message, or thesis.

Obviously, a song is not an essay. But the same principle applies in songwriting – the key to writing good verses is to give them slightly different topics, but to make sure those topics are related to your song's main message.

And that's why creating a verse masterplan is such a powerful strategy. It makes sure you don't give everything away in your first verse. It helps you reserve some fresh, new ideas for your second verse. And most importantly, it gives you a definite goal to work towards when you write the lyric of all of your verses.

That means a verse masterplan can be as simple as having a different topic focus for each verse. So in a motivational 'chin up' song, you might focus the first verse on a particular positive story. Then the second verse could add another positive story. Or in a song that says 'I love you', the first verse might focus on your first impressions when you met the person the song is about, then the second you might focus on something more intimate or more important you noticed about them more recently.

And that's basically how this works – you're trying to brainstorm a handful of specific themes or subtopics related to your song's big idea to focus each of your verses around.

And the 'specific' part is really important, by the way. As we'll talk about later, details and specifics are what brings a lyric to life – 'dusty old shoes' are much more interesting and much easier to write about than just 'some shoes'. And 'the night we met' is a much stronger verse subtopic than 'all the nights we've spent together'.

So have a think about what could work for your song idea. What subtopics feel important or worth exploring? What background ideas would help you explore and expand on your song's main message?

See where these questions take you. Invent some background or details related to your song idea if you need to. But if you need any pointers, here are a few tried-and-tested ways of differentiating your first and second verses in a really clear way:

- Write a first verse about a specific event or period of time, then a second verse about a later event or period of time.

- Write a first verse focused on 'you', then a second verse focused on 'me'. (Or vice versa.)

- Write a first verse about something that happened in a specific location, then a second verse set in a different location.

- Write a first verse about who someone is on the surface, or at a first impression, then a second verse that digs deeper into who they are or what they're feeling on the inside.

- If your song's a duet, write a first verse from one singer's perspective, then a second verse from the other singer's perspective. (This is a classic tactic for duets.)

Again, these are just five great ways of creating a good verse masterplan. They're not the only ways, and you might be able to think of some others that suit the song you're writing. But if in doubt, these five are strong verse masterplan formats to fall back on any time you might need them.

Plus, what's great about a lot of the examples I gave you is that the second verses progress beyond the first – they go deeper, or they tell the next part of the song's story. They give you the sense that the second verse lyric moves forward – not just sideways – compared to the first. That works well because even if you want your song to be centered around a single idea, it's always good to make your audience feel like you're exploring that idea more deeply as the song goes on.

But however you decide to do it for your particular song idea, spend some time now coming up with your own verse masterplan. And while verse masterplans work for songs with any number of verses, for now you obviously just want to find two strong, different but related subtopics that you could focus your verses on.

Then write your verse masterplan down somewhere – and you'll be able to use it to write your song's first verse lyric.

CREATE A VERSE MASTERPLAN

- Try to come up with a specific subtopic or theme for each of your two verses that are both related somehow to your song's big idea.
- It can help to come up with subtopics or themes that feel like they progress – but at the very least, just make sure you come up with ideas that are related but different.

WRITE THE FIRST VERSE LYRIC

So that's the first step in crafting two verse lyrics that are different enough to be interesting and that keep your song moving forward. Now it's time to take that first step and turn it into a full first verse lyric.

Pretty much everything we talked about when writing your chorus lyric applies here too, only now you don't have all of those repetitions of your lyrical hook to structure your lyric around. So in this part we're going to have to dive a bit deeper into how to come up with lyrics that rhyme, make sense and say what you want them to say.

As usual, there's no quick trick or formula to avoid working out your lyric by trial and error, line by line. But also as usual, a little bit of preparation is the key to make this trial-and-error creative wizardry as easy as possible. Lyrics rarely start to flow until you've done enough groundwork to earn it –

and in this case that means generating tons of potential ideas you could use in your lyric before you really get to work on it.

So that's where we'll start.

Generating Lyric Ideas: Free Writing

One of the first big challenges of writing good lyrics is figuring out exactly what you're trying to say. And that might sound weird – you might think you always know what you're trying to say.

But if you've ever sat down to write about an idea – even one you know a lot about – then spent most of your time staring at the wall and drawing a complete blank, you'll know what I'm talking about.

That's because half the time, writers write to *find out* what they have to say, not just to say it. Sometimes creativity is more discovery than invention, like you're trying to uncover all these great ideas that are already out there, just waiting to be found, whenever you decide to go looking for them.

So a great first step in writing a verse lyric is to try figure out what the lyric could say. You're going to forget for a moment that you're even writing a lyric at all – and not worry about rhyme, lyric structure, syllable patterns and stresses, or anything like that – and just get writing.

This is a common technique called **free writing** – which as you might expect, is just writing freely, without stopping, without censoring or editing yourself, to help you find out what you have to say on a specific topic or idea.

And sure, if you've got a strong verse masterplan and you feel confident about diving into the actual writing, it's possible to skip this step. But if writers often write to figure out what they have to say, and not just to say it, free writing is a really great way to discover things you could say on a topic that you probably wouldn't have thought of otherwise. And that's why free writing is another really powerful technique to have at your fingertips for any time you need it – even if you've been writing for years.

Here's how it works:

First, go back to your verse masterplan, take your focus for your first verse and put it somewhere important. Write it in big letters right in front of you. Tattoo it on your forearm. Crochet it into a banana. Whatever.

Second, try to put yourself in the shoes of the person who's singing your song – whether that's you, a specific other person, a band or artist, a narrator, or whoever.

Then finally, set a timer for something like 10 to 15 minutes – it could be longer or shorter, but 10 minutes is a good goal for more experienced writers, and 15 if you want to give yourself some extra time. Start the timer and just start to write from your singer's perspective about your song's main topic or message, without stopping, without editing, in free prose, until the time is up.

Don't worry if your ideas feel random or disjointed. Don't worry if you end up cutting yourself off mid-paragraph or even mid-sentence. (That's what happens when you write freely without editing or censoring yourself.) Just try to connect with the truth of the person inside your song, through the specific focus you came up with in your verse masterplan. What does your singer have to say? What's their message? What do they want everyone to know?

Then, after 10 to 15 minutes, you'll probably end up with something that looks a bit like this:

MASTERPLAN IDEA: First date, being nervous

So yeah, I came into the restaurant and I was so nervous. It'd been a while since I'd been on a first date and from your profile you looked like a really interesting person. So I was thinking 'what will he think of me?' Was I dressed OK? Was my lipstick a mess?

But then ~~he~~ you came in and I felt a lot better. You just had this big warm smile that put me at ease. You were running a few minutes late. At first I panicked because I thought maybe you were standing me up, but you said it was just the traffic and honestly the freeway is always pretty messed up at this time of night.

...

My version is probably a bit shorter than what you'll come up with in 10 to 15 minutes, but you get the idea. And as you'll see in my example, some of what comes out won't be that great. That's what happens when you let your mind wander around a topic without really thinking it through.

But the beauty of letting your mind write freely is that some of what you come up with will be gold. Maybe it'll be raw, unpolished gold – but that's still gold.

You'll come up with tons of specific ideas you can build into a finished lyric – specific ideas that especially ring true to your song's situation or idea. You can see in my example that I've already started coming up with some useful specifics about why this singer was nervous about her first date, what was running through her mind while she was waiting, and how her date put her at ease. And those are the exact kind of details you'll want in the next step.

And, by the way, one of the reasons free writing is so powerful – even for experienced writers – is that it's a way of coming up with great ideas you didn't even know you had inside. (Again, because creativity is discovery, right?) It gives your creative brain the opportunity to do its thing in a no-pressure situation, so that later you can let the more analytical and crafty side of your brain shape the ideas it came up with into something more polished. Which is exactly why, if in doubt, a free write is a great first step when you start work on a new lyric.

Generating Lyric Ideas: The Idea Brainstorm

Now that you've got some raw material or basic ideas for your first verse lyric, it's time to start refining and polishing those ideas a bit. Because, again, that'll put you in a really strong position when it's time to write your first verse lyric.

So this next stage is a lyric idea brainstorm. It's still pretty low-pressure, but unlike a free write, it comes with more of a specific structure.

In each idea brainstorm you're trying to collect a ton of specific words, phrases and entire lines that expand on your verse's focus or theme and that would feel at home in this particular lyric. You'll be able to lift a lot of these directly from the free write you just did, but you might come up with some others independently too.

It's really up to you how you organize your lyric idea brainstorms, but there are four specific types of ideas I recommend you focus on:

- **Interesting words or phrases** – To explore your verse 1 lyric masterplan idea, you'll want to use specific words, ideas and images related to that idea. So if your masterplan idea was 'nervous first date' then words and phrases like 'panic', 'reassured', 'so nervous' and 'big warm smile' are a great start. If it helps, engage all five senses to give you even more ideas – don't just think about things that can be seen and heard, but about smells, temperature, taste, anything like that.

- **Interesting rhymes** – Since you'll want to include some rhymes in your verse lyric, it's a good idea to start brainstorming some now. Obviously the more related they are to your first verse's focus or theme, the better – 'opal' and 'Constantinople' are a fun pair of rhymes but probably aren't relevant to your song's big idea. One of the best ways to do this is to take one of the words or phrases you just came up with and see what rhymes they lead to – so 'date' might lead to 'wait' and 'late', and 'big warm smile' might lead to 'for a while' and 'dial' and 'mile'. (Yes, rhyming phrases are as good as individual rhyming words. And what's great about the examples I just gave you is that they're not just any rhymes – they also fit within the world and topic focus of this verse.)

- **Potential opening lines** – It's a good idea to open each verse (and the first verse especially) with a strong, dramatic or attention-grabbing line. So it's a good idea to brainstorm a few promising options now – lines that set the scene for the song or make its topic ultra clear, or that just sound interesting, emotional or intriguing. These could be lines like 'I'd be lying if I said I was calm' or 'I'd been nervous all day'.

- **Potential final lines** – Just like the opening line of a verse is important, the final line is key to 'pivoting' the verse neatly into the chorus that comes immediately afterwards. This is a slightly more advanced technique, but one great strategy for lyric writing is to give yourself a specific line or idea to aim for at the end. And since you already know the first line of your chorus lyric, that might help you come up with something that feels like it lifts or pivots into that line. Sometimes you come up with something generic – 'I just want you to know...' – or something more specific to the situation – 'You walked in and everything changed...' Generally, good final lines in verses have the feeling of pointing somewhere new – they should feel like they end with a colon that points right to the first line of the chorus.

As I said, it's completely up to you how you organize all of these ideas. Some people like to fill a blank page or twenty with different ideas as they come up with them. Some people prefer one page for each different category of ideas. Some people like to write ideas around the edge of a giant piece of paper so they can then write the actual lyric in the middle later. Some people type their ideas in a document or note on their phone or computer – but if you're anything like me, I usually find myself working much more creatively when I'm working old-school with pen and paper and not on a screen.

So I'll leave it to you to do your lyric idea brainstorm in the way that feels best for you – but if you want a blank template to copy out and fill in, there's one on the page opposite.

Unlike with free writing, in this part of the process there's no time limit. Your only job is to spend as much time as you need to come up with more ideas than you could ever use in your lyric – maybe something like thirty interesting phrases, twenty pairs of good rhymes, and at least three or four

LYRIC IDEA BRAINSTORM – VERSE 1

Verse Theme or Focus: _____

Opening lines

Interesting rhymes

Interesting words / phrases

Closing lines / Pivot lines

potential opening and closing lines. Like always, you're trying to give yourself plenty of options so you can pick out the best ones later.

You can come up with these ideas in any order or any way you like. One trick I often use to balance finding interesting words and phrases with finding interesting rhymes is to let my mind wander between both categories, wherever it goes. So I might start with related words like 'shoes', 'hair' and 'red dress', which leads me down a miniature rhyme rabbit hole of 'dress', 'mess', 'less' and 'stress', which leads on to words like 'anxious', 'nervous', 'tense', 'heartbeat' and so on. You get the idea.

Again, you're welcome to use a rhyming dictionary or sites like rhymezone.com to help you find rhymes if you want to – especially when you've come up with a great word or phrase but don't know what to rhyme it with. But like I said before, you want to make sure you filter out only the words that rhyme *and* say something that's related to your theme or focus for your first verse. (Plus, it's always a good idea to stretch your rhyming muscles by coming up with rhymes on your own from time to time too.)

And that's pretty much it – the final step in generating some lyric ideas before you start to craft them into a finished lyric.

And if you came here because of the rockstar image some people have of songwriting but you're starting to face the cold, hard reality that a big part of lyric writing is just making lists, it's OK. A big part of lyric writing really is making lists. I won't lie. But, as you know, some solid preparation is nearly always the trick to writing something great.

So get those lists made, compadre, and once that's done we'll get crafting your actual first verse lyric.

BRAINSTORM SOME LYRIC IDEAS

- **Spend plenty of time generating lyric ideas you could use in your first verse lyric.**
- **Focus on finding interesting words and phrases, interesting rhymes and potential opening and closing lines related to your first verse's theme or focus.**
- **If you need to, start out with a free write from the perspective of the person (or people) singing your song.**

Write the First Verse Lyric

OK. Nice work. Now it's time to turn all of those great ideas you generated into a complete first verse lyric.

As I said in Part 5, I recommend you write eight lyric lines that fill 16 measures in your verses. And for simplicity, I recommend you also stick with an XXAXAXBXB rhyme scheme in your verse lyric. (Though if you're feeling confident and want to try something else, you can go ahead and try one of the other options I mentioned in the rhyme toolbox starting on page 34.)

So just like with writing your chorus lyric, a good first step is to mark out the number of lines of your lyric on a sheet of lined paper or in a document on your screen:

1
2
3
4
5
6
7
8

And from here, I'll be honest: results may vary. I'm going to try my best to focus on the important principles, as always, but the way you go from a few blank lines to a finished lyric probably won't be exactly the same as mine. But, as always, if you use the ideas we talk about, and keeping trying out a ton of different things, your lyric will come together in its own way eventually.

So now, if you go back to your lyric idea brainstorm – which by now should be covered in more ideas than you could ever use in this verse – you'll probably find something kind of magical has started to happen. Among all the different ideas you put down, some will start standing out to you. They'll start looking like the best or most interesting ideas on the page – and obviously they're the ones to focus on using first.

That said, there are three starting tactics I especially recommend for getting started on a verse lyric. So if in doubt, it's a good idea to start with one – or more – of these:

- Pick out a strong opening line – start with something strong that grabs our attention and draws us into your lyric, then let the rest of the lyric flow from there.

- Pick out a strong closing or pivot line – give yourself an ultimate goal or final idea to get to, then let the rest of the lyric build towards it.

- Pick some strong rhymes for the ends of your rhyming lines – like lines 2 and 4, then 6 and 8 in an XAXAXBXB rhyme scheme – and build your lyric around that.

Sometimes one of these techniques will work better than the others – though you won't always find out which will work best for your song until you try them. But to show you how you can use each tactic I'm going to build a verse lyric using a combination of all three.

We'll stick with the 'I'm on a first date and I was nervous' idea we've been working with in this part.

So as a first step, I might come up with something like this:

1 I'd be lying if I said I was calm
2
3
4
5
6   (more / sure / explore?)
7
8 But then you walked in the door...

You can probably see what I did here.

First, I came up with opening line that I thought was strong – it's emotional, it's kind of dramatic, and it makes it clear right away that the theme of this verse is 'being nervous' – by re-phrasing an idea from my free write.

Second, I took one of the ideas for a closing line to create line 8. I actually rephrased 'But you walked in the room and everything changed' because that felt too long for one line. And I also switched 'in the door' for 'in the room' because I figured 'door' has tons more rhyming options than 'room' – and sometimes in lyric writing it's good to go with whatever's going to make your life easier.

Finally, since I know I want line 6 to end with something that rhymes with 'door' at the end of line 8, I penciled in three rhymes that felt promising there – even though I don't really know what that line is going to say yet.

And I should add – none of the lyric I've written so far is set in stone. It's just my first shot at putting something together that has shape and structure. If it works out, great, I'll keep it. But as I keep writing, if it looks like a dead end, I'm not going to take it personally if I have to tear this plan down and trying something else. (OK, I'll take it a little bit personally.)

But for now, I'm optimistic it'll work out, and just like we did in Part 3 with a chorus lyric, I'm going to start building around what I've got already to see what happens.

Since we have lines 1 and 8, two good next lines to try might be lines 2 and 7 to complete those pairs. So I might try something like this:

1 I'd be lying if I said I was calm
2 While I sat there waiting for you.
3 'Dinner at eight, don't be late...'
4 But then I'm waiting on you to come through.
                              (too / through / new?)
5
6   (more / sure / explore?)
7
8 But then you walked in the door...

And wow – I actually got carried away and found a bit of a flow for the first four lines. I started with line 2, obviously, trying to continue line 1 with something that made sense and followed on from the verse's first thought. Then a quick conversational flashback – with a nifty 'eight' and 'late' **internal rhyme**, within a single line – came to me for line 3.

Then, I found a way to continue that thought onto line 4, ending in a neat 'ooh' rhyme to match 'you'. (Though I kept a few other rhymes in there, just in case I change my mind and want to rewrite this part of the lyric later.)

And honestly, I got pretty lucky this time – lyric lines don't always come that quickly or that easily. But by starting with the line 1 I'd penciled in, I used that to lead me to a line 2 I liked. And then I used the rhyme I'd put at the end of line 2 to give me a rhyme to aim for in line 4. On a bad day, it would have taken me a lot longer and a lot more tries to make it work, but that's still the exact strategy I'd have tried.

This time round, I didn't give you a completed lyric idea brainstorm that I could have gotten these ideas from, but let's assume I took all of line 1 directly from that brainstorm, then built the rest of the lyric from there.

Plus, let's assume I came up with the two rhymes 'wait' and 'late' in my idea brainstorm. As you can see, 'wait' found its way into lines 2 and 4 – not as a rhyme – and the actual internal rhymes I used in line 3 are 'eight' and 'late'. But that's actually a nice demonstration for how this works – you'll often be able to lift some ideas straight from your brainstorm, but you'll have to invent or adapt others on the fly to make them work.

In fact, that's kind of the key to lyric writing in general – having a plan but being able to improvise around the plan when you need to. Because while it's not impossible I could have come up with that neat 'eight' and 'late' internal rhyme without doing an idea brainstorm or any other groundwork, taking some time to do that stage properly will always increase the chances that you'll write your best lyrics.

Next, I could try to find something for line 7, but instead I'm going to try to keep my flow going by writing something for lines 5 and 6. And since I penciled in a few '-ore' rhymes in line 6 already, that's a nice head start.

So, after spending a couple of minutes phrasing options for line 6 around the rhymes I've already got, here's one version I could use:

5
6 [...] I had to know more.
7
8 But then you walked in the door...

And a second one that's a bit different but could still work:

5
6 [...] I felt so unsure.
7
8 But then you walked in the door...

All I've done here is combine the rhymes I already had with two of the concepts from my very first free write – the idea of being intrigued about someone on a date, and the idea of feeling nervous and uncertain.

And the truth is, I could make either of these options work. But my gut instinct is to try and make the intrigue and curiosity version work. Maybe your instincts are telling you something different, and that's great – but for me, focusing on the curiosity of the moment sounds more interesting and upbeat than going on about feeling anxious. So I'm going to go for the phrase 'I had to know more' in line 6 and see where it takes me.

First, I'm going to try extending that line into 'I knew I had to know more'. I think my subconscious brain likes it because it sneaks another 'ooh' rhyme in the middle of that line – a quick throwback to the 'you' and 'through' rhyme before, plus the 'you' at the end of line 5 – but it also makes line 6 a similar length to the other lines I've got so far. (And as I said in Part 4, that usually makes giving the lyric a melody much easier.)

From there, I'll need something in line 5 that leads nicely into line 6 – something that vaguely says 'when I first heard about you', or 'when I first saw your online profile'. Or, if we're OK with making the singer sound more superficial, it could be something like 'when I first saw your face'.

5 When I first heard all about you,
6 I knew I had to know more,
7 Still, I sat there counting the minutes
8 But then you walked in the door...

And voilà. It works. It's complete.

In my first free write, it sounded like these two people met online, but in the actual lyric, I've made it sound like they were introduced by a friend because that felt stronger somehow. (That's another example of taking the ideas in your free write or brainstorm but adapting them as you write.)

Then, in line 7, to avoid repeating a phrase like 'waiting for you' another time, I tried to pick an image or idea that says that, only in a different way. I toyed with 'watching the clock tick' or 'checking my phone' but decided 'counting the minutes' sounded best.

And actually, looking at it now, I'm going to change the 'but' in the last line – which feels kind of heavy-handed now – into 'until' instead (which creates another neat bonus rhyme with 'still' in the line before).

And that's it, a complete eight-line first verse lyric:

1 I'd be lying if I said I was calm
2 While I sat there waiting for you.
3 'Dinner at eight, don't be late...'
4 But then I'm waiting on you to come through.
5 When I first heard all about you,
6 I knew I had to know more,
7 Still, I sat there counting the minutes
8 Until you walked in the door...

And if you were wondering, yes, I only used a tiny proportion of the ideas I came up with earlier. And yes, that's completely normal. As you know, it's worth coming up with lots of potential ideas so you can pick out the best ones. But in lyric writing, you often don't have a ton of space to make your point – so you often want to end up with just a few strong ideas that say what you want to say, so you can put them proudly center stage.

So there you go – that's the process, and a lot of the ideas behind it, that went into writing this particular 8-line verse.

Again – and I can't stress this enough – your experience of writing your first verse lyric probably won't look exactly like mine. You might find a completely different tactic or different order to turn the best ideas in your idea brainstorm into a finished lyric. And that's great. That's how it works.

But whatever your experience looks like, the best way to start writing a lyric is to begin with one or more strong lines, then try building everything else around them, line by line, in whatever way you can.

And then, if that doesn't go to plan, you can always try a different first or last line, or a different rhyme or phrase – or even a completely different strategy or tactic – and it'll all come together soon enough.

And if you ever feel really stuck on a particular lyric, it can help to try working in focused 20- or 30-minute chunks, and if it's still not flowing take a break and come back to it later. Often the thing you were stressing about won't seem so complicated when you come back to it. Plus, sometimes your subconscious will treat you by solving something tricky while you're away – but only if you've spent some time trying to fix it consciously first.

If you've been writing a while and want to push yourself – and your lyrics – a bit further, I've included a toolbox with a few more advanced ideas over the page. But either way, I'll say it again – writing lyrics is hard. So keep going. Keep trying different words, phrases and rhymes until you've got a verse lyric that you're happy with.

And then, once you do, we'll look at how to complete your first verse by adding a vocal melody to the lyric you've just written.

 ## WRITE THE FIRST VERSE LYRIC

- **Spend plenty of time generating lyric ideas with a quick free write and then a longer brainstorming session of words and phrases related to your first verse topic.**
- **Then try to craft the best and most interesting ideas you brainstormed into a complete first verse lyric.**
- **Stick to a simple rhyme scheme like XAXAXBXB, try to include plenty of specifics in your lyric, and keep it as naturally conversational as you can.**

 **TOOLBOX**

EXTRA LYRIC WRITING TIPS

Include Plenty of Specifics

Lyrics thrive on specifics. Sometimes it can feel weird to choose something like 'one Tuesday morning' over just 'one morning' – because you might wonder whether that level of detail really matters. But it does. Including specific details makes your lyric feel more real.

Obviously there's a limit to that – 'one Tuesday morning at precisely 7.13am and fourteen seconds' sounds ridiculous. But the more specifics you include in your lyric, the more strongly it'll conjure up a world or image in your listener's imagination. That's another reason why spending some time generating some specific lyric ideas before you start writing is so important.

Make Your Song's Situation Clear in the First Four Lines

That said, you don't have space to clarify every single detail in a song lyric, because song lyrics are usually only a few hundred words long. So sometimes lyric writing is a balance between painting a really detailed picture and leaving some things more open-ended. But if there's one place you want your lyric to be especially clear, it's right at the beginning.

You'll give us more information as the song goes on, but you usually want your audience to feel sure that they understand what the song is about – who it's about, what's going on, or where it's happening – as soon as possible. So it's worth making sure you're not keeping anyone guessing by making the basics of your song's situation clear within the first four lines – or even the first two.

Keep It Conversational

I mentioned this when we talked about how to choose a lyrical hook, but it's a good principle of lyric writing in general: a good lyric sounds conversational, like it's coming from a person speaking.

That means it's a good idea to use slang or contractions – like 'can't' instead of 'cannot'. It means it's OK to use incomplete sentences – like 'Dinner at eight, don't be late', like I did in my example earlier. But whatever you write, the acid test is always whether it sounds like a real person speaking.

Stick to the Same Perspective (Tense and Voice)

I've spoken a lot in this book about making sure your song comes from one big idea or vision. And one common thing that trips up new writers is switching the tense – past, present or future – or voice – I/we, you, he/she/it/they – mid-song without good reason.

That might sound kind of obvious – and there are a few good reasons to switch your song's perspective in the middle of a song – but if you wrote your chorus in the past tense and then wrote your first verse in the present tense, you want to be sure that you meant for it to happen, that it was a definite choice and not an accident.

Don't Hit the Nail on the Head All the Time

In Part 2 we talked about how some lyrical hooks are pretty direct and some are more metaphorical or suggestive. That's true of lyrics in general – sometimes direct lyrics work well but you usually don't want to hit the nail on the head all that time. That's because asking your audience to a bit of work to understand your lyric usually engages them in a much more active way.

It's one reason I opened my example verse lyric with 'I'd be lying if I said I was calm...' instead of 'OMG, I WAS SO NERVOUS!!!'. This is often called 'show don't tell' – the idea that it's better to describe someone shivering than just to say 'she was cold'. Of course, telling has its place in songwriting too. It's just that telling *all* the time gets boring, and – as I say in *The Art of Songwriting* – you want to include plenty of showing to make the telling more compelling.

[PART 7]
WRITE THE VERSE MELODY AND CREATE A VERSE BUILD

[PART 7]

WRITE THE VERSE MELODY AND CREATE A VERSE BUILD

In this part... | How to give your verse lyric a melody, and make your verse groove build into the chorus.

Now you've got the foundation of your verses done – your verse chords and groove, and a first verse lyric – it's time to finish crafting your verses' music with a vocal melody and a nice build into the chorus.

WRITE THE VERSE MELODY

Again, there's good news – there's nothing radically different between writing verse vocal melodies and chorus vocal melodies. So like before, I recommend you stick with this process:

- Keep the same time signature and tempo you chose before. (While it's true that some songs change keys between sections – including using a different key for their verses and choruses – songwriters almost never change time signature or tempo between song sections.)

- Then, make a rhythmic sketch that fits the first verse lyric you wrote in Part 6. You usually want to give each lyric line the same number of measures you did in your chorus – probably two. And again, try to bear the principles of good prosody in mind – you're aiming to give your lyric a rhythm that sounds, more or less, like the way you'd speak those words.

- From there, you can turn that rhythmic sketch into a full melody. Like before, it's a good idea to focus each measure of your melody on one or more notes in the chord underneath. And like before, it's a good idea to build your melody in complete vocal phrases. While you do that, you want to try to find opportunities to create repetition of entire phrases or parts of phrases.

That said, there are a couple of subtle ways that writing verse melodies *isn't* quite like writing chorus melodies. So if you want a bit of an extra challenge in this part, there are two extra things you can think about.

First, while chorus melodies tend to be more showy and even dramatic – like they're making a big statement – verse melodies tend to be more casual and conversational. That's because it's the job of your choruses to make a big statement – to say what your song is about really directly – while the verses are more about setting up your song's story, giving us some background details related to your song's big idea and often, helping us get familiar with your singer. So if you can write a verse vocal melody that feels more casual and even understated, that usually works well.

Second, because the job of each verse is to lead up and into the chorus that comes after it – we'll talk more about this soon – it's a good idea to think about how your verse melody connects into your chorus melody.

For starters, you usually want your verse melody to end in roughly the same vocal **register**, or pitch area of the voice, as your chorus melody begins. There are exceptions, but you mostly want to make each verse feel like it connects into the chorus after it, and not like you just plonked those two sections side by side. (Again, more on that soon.)

And speaking of register, as a general rule, songs often stick to a generally lower register in their verses to their chorus. That's another way you can make your choruses feel like your song's big event and your verses more like a warm-up act. So if in doubt, don't be afraid to start your verse vocal melody in a fairly low register, and focus on using generally lower notes at first – and then you can start to use some higher pitches later on in the verse and into the chorus after it.

And that's about it – that's all there is to think about before you dive in and write your verse melody.

So go get your hands dirty again. Go play around with a ton of different melodic and rhythmic ideas to see what you like. Like last time, if you want to set a metronome, beat or loop of your verses' chord progression playing while you figure out a vocal melody over the top, that's a great strategy.

And also like last time, once you've got a verse melody you're happy with, find a way to record or notate it – both because you'll want a definitive version recorded so you don't forget or lose it, and because you'll need that melody on hand when it comes to writing your second verse lyric in the next part.

WRITE THE VERSE MELODY

- Like you did with your chorus melody, write a verse vocal melody that fits your first verse lyric and the verse chord progression you wrote.
- It's a good idea to start with a rhythmic sketch again, then craft a finished vocal melody from there, thinking in phrases and trying to include plenty of melodic repetition.
- Keep your verse melody more relaxed and conversational than your chorus melody – and try to finish your verse melody in a register that leads nicely into the chorus.

CREATE A VERSE BUILD

Next, it's time to talk about a concept that's not quite new – we've touched on it a few times already – but is worth thinking about in a bit more detail. That's right – we're going to look at how to connect the different sections of your song effectively, and specifically how to make sure all of your song's verses lead nicely into each chorus.

One thing you've probably noticed when you listen to a song – or any piece of music – is that some parts of the song sound more exciting than others. Just like in a good movie, a song has highs, lows, fast-paced bits, more relaxed bits – and listening to it takes you on a miniature journey.

In fact, if you had to summarize what most verse-chorus songs do in a nifty graph, you'd find they do something like this:

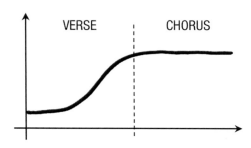

Or like this:

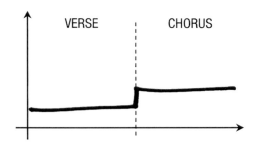

Or even something like this:

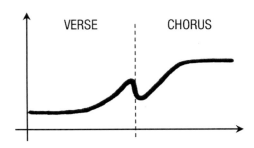

But on the other hand, you'll almost never find a verse-chorus song that does this:

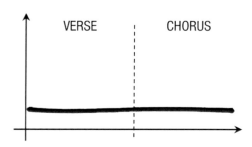

And it would be pretty weird if a verse-chorus song did this:

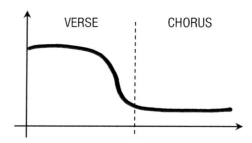

But hold on a second. What exactly is the mystery quantity on the vertical axis? Joy? Hi-hats per second? The number of times the word 'me' is pronounced more like 'mehhh'?

I hinted at it earlier, and you might have a hunch already, but it's the level of musical intensity or energy in your song. It's the way different sections of your song say 'just sit tight, something really interesting is coming', or 'YO, LISTEN UP – this is the most important part of the song', plus everything in between. And it's the way your song's music sounds more or less exciting in different sections to keep your listener engaged in your song's overall shape or journey.

Because just like part of the fun of going on a trip of a lifetime or to an amazing festival is the anticipation – the time between buying your tickets and actually getting to do what you paid for – in a song, part of what keeps you interested is the feeling that something exciting is coming.

In a verse-chorus structure, the most exciting and most important part of the structure – the structure's main event – is usually the song's chorus.

We've talked about this a lot – it's the idea that your chorus is where you really hammer home your song's message and make sure people are paying attention. But the rest of the song isn't just a break from that – you use those sections to build up to the next chorus or take us away from the chorus somehow.

That's why, as you saw from the nifty explanatory graphs on the previous page, the chorus is usually the most intense, energetic and exciting section in a verse-chorus structure, and one important job of each verse is to build in intensity and energy so that when the chorus lands, we really know about it.

So how does this work in practice? How do you control the levels of intensity or energy in your song?

As always, there are a handful of different ways to affect your song's intensity levels – whatever instruments or technology you're writing with. But here are five of the best:

To increase a song's intensity or energy level:

- Make the groove busier rhythmically – maybe by strumming or playing chords at a faster rate, or by including more notes in your percussion track.

- Increase the overall **dynamics** – or volume – of the groove.

- Add extra tracks or parts – maybe an extra synth track or having more ideas going on at once in your piano track.

- Write fuller or thicker chords – writing chords with more notes in them.

- Write a groove that spreads out over a wider **range** – that uses some higher or lower pitches, and often both.

That means that most of the time, controlling the level of intensity in your song is about managing its grooves – how busy they are, how loud they are, and how full they sound. But especially, most of this is about managing your song's **texture** – the number of instrumental parts, and how they work together – as your song progresses.

That's why when it came to writing your verse groove I suggested you kept it as small and chilled as possible – so you could make your texture busier, raise the overall dynamic level, or add extra or fuller parts later, so that your song feels like it's building somewhere.

And ditto, that's the reason you generally want to keep your vocal melody in a lower register in your verses than your choruses – it helps reinforce the idea that your choruses are your song's main event. In fact, with verse builds it's usually a good idea to rely on two or more different techniques to create an increase in intensity – because that makes the effect stronger than just using one technique alone.

So have a think about how these ideas apply to the song you're writing. Sometimes it's enough just to use a slightly more intense or energetic groove in your choruses than your verses – that make your choruses feel like a bigger deal than your verses. (I represented this earlier in the 'blocky' second graph I gave you.) But often, it sounds better to make your song's intensity rise more gradually in your verses – and towards the second half of each verse in particular.

Sometimes these changes can be pretty subtle – your chorus doesn't have to be the most intense, energetic 16 measures of music you've ever written, and your verse doesn't have to be the most low-key. But it's worth taking some time now to make sure you're happy with the way your verses and choruses in your song work together – not just as sections side by side, but as a partnership that takes us on a mini adventure.

This might mean making some changes to your verse groove, your chorus groove, or both. It might mean making some subtle changes in the second half of your verse groove but leaving the first half intact.

But however you do it, like always, you're trying to come up with something that *feels* right – that *feels* like it creates that little rise and fall you find in virtually every verse and chorus in virtually every verse-chorus song ever.

If you need some inspiration – or want to hear first-hand how this works – it's not a bad idea to go listen to some of your favorite songs and try to figure out how they approach this fundamental idea. That'll help you understand how what I've said about creating a verse build works in practice, and maybe help you discover even more techniques for controlling your song's intensity level.

But either way, as always, have a play around with your song. Use what you know and what instruments and technology you've got to apply this idea and see what you can come up with.

Then, once you've done that, we'll start thinking about your song's second verse lyric.

CREATE A VERSE BUILD

- Spend some time making sure your song's verses feel like they build in intensity into your choruses.
- This might mean writing thicker or faster chords, adding extra tracks or parts, or increasing the dynamics in your verses' grooves.
- You could also tweak your song's chorus grooves to make sure your chorus is your song's main event.

[PART 8]

WRITE THE SECOND VERSE LYRIC AND START PUTTING YOUR SONG TOGETHER

[PART 8]

WRITE THE SECOND VERSE LYRIC AND START PUTTING YOUR SONG TOGETHER

In this part... | *How to write the second verse lyric – and how to start putting all your song sections together.*

Now it's time to think about your second verse lyric – and thanks to your hard work on your verse masterplan, there shouldn't be any second verse curse in sight.

Then, after you've got a second verse, we'll spend some time putting everything you've written so far together in one place, including creating a professional-looking lyric sheet and finding some way to notate or record your entire song.

And yes, that means you're finally on the homeward stretch. So let's keep going.

WRITE THE SECOND VERSE LYRIC

The good news is that, other than the different topic focus, the process for coming up with your second verse lyric is pretty much the same as the one you used in your first verse. So, in short:

- Take a moment to write down your second verse lyric's focus or theme somewhere prominent – because again, you want your entire second verse lyric to spring from it.

- Then try a quick free write around that focus or theme to help you figure out what your second verse could be saying. Use those ideas to create a new lyric idea brainstorm – focus on coming up with interesting words and phrases, interesting rhymes, and potential opening and closing lines, and as usual, try to come up with more ideas than you'll actually need.

- Finally, once you've got plenty of ideas to work with, you can craft the strongest of them into a complete lyric. And that's it.

Like before, this process can take plenty of time – so don't be tempted to rush the free writing and brainstorming stages. Chances are, those stages are where you'll come up with some of your most exciting ideas.

It's also a good idea to keep the structure and shape of your first verse lyric in your second verse lyric. By that I mean keeping the same number of lines – since both lyrics will take the same melody – and keeping the same rhyme scheme, if you can.

Plus, since both verse lyrics will take the same, or a similar, melody, you generally want the number of syllables in your second verse to match your first verse, more or less. Different songwriters have different attitudes to this – and yes, trying to write something that matches in your second verse usually makes the process harder – but that kind of regularity and consistency tends to have a really positive effect on your listener.

You can make some minor changes – maybe adding or taking away a syllable or two – like this:

(You can play 'spot the difference' if you want to see exactly how I changed the melody the second time so it fits the new lyric – but if you listen, you'll hear how I kept the gist of the first verse melody intact.)

But in general, if your second verse lyric is going to fit your verse melody, you don't want to make too many changes. Sometimes you have to try a lot of different versions of a lyric line before you find a way to say what you want to say to fit a specific melody – but if you keep trying, you'll find a great solution soon enough.

That said, you can also use that regularity to your advantage when you write your second verse. Like if your first verse opens with the word 'hey' to grab your listeners' attention, you could start your second verse with something like 'oh' to create the same effect.

Or, if you came up with a killer final line in your first verse lyric, there might be a way to rephrase or vary that line to create something fresh but familiar in your second verse. So if you end your first verse with the pivot line 'I really need you to know…', you could end your second verse with a pivot line like 'So listen up while I say…', or 'I wish you'd listen to me…', or 'Please hear what I have to say…'.

Also, it's your call, but I recommend you try and find different-sounding rhymes in your second verse – so if you rhymed 'me' and 'be' the first time, you avoid any major '-ee' rhymes in your second verse to keep things fresh.

And that's basically it. If you need to look back to Part 6 to familiarize yourself with any of the techniques we talked about there, that's not a bad idea. Otherwise, go ahead and work the same creative magic with a new verse focus or theme, and see how you can further expand the story you started telling in verse 1.

 ## WRITE THE SECOND VERSE LYRIC

- Spend some time generating tons of lyric ideas like you did for your first verse, using your second verse's topic or theme according to your verse masterplan.
- Then craft those ideas into a new verse lyric, trying to match the structure and format of your first verse as much as possible.

LYRIC IDEA BRAINSTORM – VERSE 2

Verse Theme or Focus: _____

Opening lines

Interesting rhymes

Interesting words / phrases

Closing lines / Pivot lines

START PUTTING YOUR SONG TOGETHER

Nice work. That's the bulk of your song completed – or at least, the main body of your song. So bravo.

In the final two parts of this process we'll look at adding three other sections – a bridge, intro and outro. But before we do that, it makes sense to put everything you've written so far together in one place, if you haven't already. So let's take a moment to talk about that.

Put Your Song Sections Together

First of all, putting your song together just means creating a definitive version of everything you've created so far, in the proper order, all in one place. That might be a complete recording, or a complete notated version of your song, or a single project file in your DAW.

That might sound obvious, but if you've been creating everything as separate sections, it's important you bring everything together.

And if this is your first song, you can take a step back, be super proud of what you created and move on to the next section.

But if you're a more experienced writer, now that you have your entire song in one place you might want to spend some time listening to it all in order and think about making a few tweaks to what you've written before you continue.

Specifically, here are a handful of things to consider:

- You'll want to make sure you're happy with the way your song moves between sections. For example, sometimes it makes sense to add an extra two or four measures as a breather after each chorus before it moves on to the next section. These short sections are called **turnarounds**, and they usually just repeat your chorus groove and chord progression once or twice more.

- Equally, you might want to make some minor tweaks to the music of the second verse or chorus – especially if you're working in a DAW. While it's true that your second verse and chorus are going to repeat the music of your first verse and chorus, sometimes it's a nice touch to vary them slightly the second time round. Maybe that means adding an extra synth track or some vocal 'ooh's or 'ahh's. Or tweaking the groove slightly – so it's still recognizable, but just different enough to keep your audience on their toes.

- But whatever changes you make, you want to keep them subtle – it's important that all of the repeated sections in your song sound like repetitions, and not something new. And as a general rule, when something comes back in your song it should always be either as interesting or more interesting than before, and not less. So you can add layers or add interest – or keep things the same – but you generally want to make it feel like you're building on what you've done already, not giving us all you've got then following up with something less exciting. (Again, that's all to do with how you plan out your song's levels of energy and intensity.)

And that's that. Naturally, these extra techniques won't work in every song – and songs with simple, direct repetition also work great. But they're there as options if you want to use them.

Create a Lyric Sheet for Your Song

Finally, before you move on, it's worth creating a professional-looking lyric sheet for your song. If you share your song with anyone, a good lyric sheet serves as an official version of everything you've written – and it'll also be really useful for you to see your entire song in one place.

Different writers and different genres have their own conventions for formatting lyric sheets, but most lyric sheets include all of these things:

- The entire lyric of the song.

- Some quick labels to point out the structure of the song.

- The song's title and writing credits – and, if you're sharing the song with other people, the contact details of at least one of the writers.

To show you what I mean, I've made up a quick example on the next two pages.

It's up to you whether you copy out the chorus each time. Some songwriters just write 'REPEAT CHORUS' as a shorthand after the first time it appears, but I prefer writing everything in full so you can see the song as it'll be performed.

Also, it's up to you to use punctuation at the end of your lyric lines in a way that makes sense – but remember, you can't really sing punctuation, so it's worth keeping everything as simple as possible.

And finally, sometimes you'll have to make some creative decisions about how you split your lyric onto different lines. Like I said before, the most important thing is that your lyric makes sense musically – but it's worth writing it down in a way that's as clear as possible.

A WHOLE D*MN SONG

Words and music by Ed Bell
ejbmusic@mail.com

VERSE 1

Some days in your life
Netflix just isn't enough,
So you've got to hunker down
And try something kind of tough.
Something that's a challenge
That's interesting but fun,
Like writing a new song,
And that's exactly what I've done.

CHORUS

I wrote a whole d*mn song,
It isn't very long
But I wrote the whole song
On my own.
I wrote a whole d*mn song,
So you can sing along
And I'm so proud
That I did it alone.

VERSE 2

Yeah, life can be dull,
And your job is a grind.
So you need a new outlet
For your creative mind.
'Cos everything is better
When you do it your way.
That's what writing's all about
And it's why I'm glad to say…

CHORUS

I wrote a whole d*mn song,
It isn't very long
But I wrote the whole song
On my own.
I wrote a whole d*mn song,
So you can sing along
And I'm so proud
That I did it alone.

BRIDGE

[…]

CHORUS

I wrote a whole d*mn song,
It isn't very long
But I wrote the whole song
On my own.
I wrote a whole d*mn song,
So you can sing along
And I'm so proud
That I did it alone.

(Repeat CHORUS and fade)

Oh, and also – you'll see I added a quick copyright notice at the bottom of this lyric sheet. That's good practice, and you can do the same if you like, but honestly – and especially if you're still new to songwriting – you mostly don't need to worry about someone 'stealing' your song. There's more on why in a toolbox at the end of this section on page 193.

So that's the deal with lyric sheets. And whatever kind of songs you write, it's worth creating a professional-looking lyric sheet so that you have a complete record of what you've created.

If you want to go one step further, you could find a way to write down your song's music. One simple way to do that is to add chord symbols to your lyric sheet – over the words where the chord changes – like this:

	C	F
CHORUS	I wrote a whole d*mn song,	
	Am G	
	It isn't very long	
	C	F
	But I wrote the whole song	
	Am G	
	On my own.	

If you prefer, you can write your chord progressions out separately nearby – with a new progression at the top of each section, if you need to.

Alternatively, if you have the notation skills, you can create what's called a **lead sheet** – a single staff of music with your song's vocal melody, plus its lyric and chords – like this:

(Some lead sheets just come with chord symbols – the chord names as text – without the guitar charts underneath. But I included both here.)

Alternatively, if you're writing for live instruments and you have the skills, you can also write your song out in notation – even if some parts of your song are notated roughly, or use some kind of shorthand:

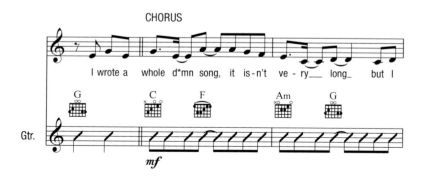

But again – notating your song's music in one of these more advanced ways is optional. At the very least, though, you want a proper lyric sheet for your song, plus some kind of complete recording – either of you performing the song, even roughly, or a version of the song in your DAW, or some kind of notated version of the song like I showed you.

And then, once you've done that, it'll be time to add the final few sections to your song.

PUT YOUR SONG TOGETHER

- Create a lyric sheet for your song so far – including your song's complete lyric plus some other important information.
- Take a moment to combine everything you've created so far in one place – either in a recording, in a file in your DAW, or in musical notation.

✖ TOOLBOX

COPYRIGHT BASICS

There are a lot of misconceptions about copyright in songwriting – and honestly, a lot of songwriters worry about it way more than they need to, especially if they're just starting out. So let's clear things up on two common misconceptions.

Nobody Is Going to Steal Your New Song (Probably)

Sure, whenever you create something new there's always the risk that someone will do something they shouldn't with it. But the chances of that happening are usually really small.

A lot of songwriters worry that someone 'in the music industry' is going to discover their song, 'steal' it and make a fortune off the back of it. And while in theory that's possible, in practice it's not common. Music industry execs are usually looking for *extremely* specific songs for their artists – songs that are tailor-made to fit the style and image they want to promote.

So even if you're writing songs to a professional standard already, the probability that someone massively dishonest comes across your song, *and* they like what you've written, *and* it happens to fit what they need perfectly, *and* they decide to go ahead with ruthlessly ripping it off to make themselves a fortune is usually pretty remote. So most of the time, you can sleep easy.

Your Song is Automatically Copyrighted the Second You Write It Down

That's right – you don't actually have to do anything to copyright a song. You don't need to register it anywhere. You don't have to get it notarized by an attorney. You don't have to sacrifice a copy of it at midnight on the night before the first full moon each February. And you definitely don't have to mail a sealed copy of it to yourself. (That's sometimes called 'poor man's copyright' – but it doesn't work anyway because you could send yourself an empty envelope and seal it up later).

All you have to do to copyright a song is to make sure it exists physically somewhere other than your brain – you just have to write it down, record it, save it as a file, or anything like that. That's it.

In some countries it's possible to register copyrighted works officially if you want to. (In the US, for example, The Library of Congress manages the national copyright registration system.) That doesn't copyright the work – because that happens automatically – but it usually makes things easier in future if you have to make a copyright claim because someone infringes on what you wrote. So it's usually only worth the expense and hassle of registering a copyright if you're going to release a song publicly or plan on seriously promoting it or shopping it around.

So in short, yes copyright and intellectual property theft are serious topics. But in general – and especially if you're still figuring songwriting out – they're not worth worrying about too much.

[PART 9]

ADD A BRIDGE

[PART 9]

ADD A BRIDGE

In this part... | A few powerful techniques for adding a contrasting bridge to your song.

So here we are – that's most of your song done. All that's left in these final two parts is to think about putting the finishing touches to your song.

The first section to think about adding is a **bridge** – sometimes also called a **release**, **middle eight** or **primary bridge**. But whatever you call it, a bridge's job is always the same: to create a contrast or escape from the world your song has already established. That's why a song's bridge usually comes after its second chorus – to break up the regular pattern of verse, chorus, verse, chorus with something new and unexpected.

There are a few different ways to create this contrast, but we'll start by focusing on the most common way – writing a 'standard' vocal bridge with a contrasting lyric and new music.

If you're new to songwriting, this is the kind of bridge I strongly recommend you write. But if you've been writing a while, I'm also going to show you how to work with two other great options – writing an instrumental bridge, or writing no bridge at all (and why, in some songs, that can be the best choice).

WRITING A 'STANDARD' VOCAL BRIDGE

So, as I said, the key to writing a good bridge is contrast – giving us something in your song that's different, that hasn't happened already, that takes us somewhere new. That means most bridges have a new lyric, new melody, a new chord progression and a new groove.

Still, like we've talked about with other song sections, you don't want your song's bridge to sound like it comes from another planet – or just another song. You want to feel like it belongs to the same world, only a different part of it.

That's sometimes a delicate balancing act, but it means your bridge's lyric is going to be new, yet still related to your song's overall idea. And it means your bridge's music will sound fresh but like it belongs to the same musical world as the rest of your song.

So let's talk about how that works in practice.

Find a Contrasting Lyric Perspective

The strategy to writing a good bridge lyric is pretty simple – **you want it to add a new and different perspective to what your song has talked about so far.**

If your second verse is supposed to feel like a step forward from your first verse, your bridge should feel like a step to the side – like it puts your song's message in a slightly different light, or gives it some extra context.

Now is a good time to remind yourself of your song's big idea, as well as revisit your verse masterplan. In your bridge, you're going to take your masterplan one step further – only not with something that feels like a continuation or extension, but like a contrast.

As usual, there are lots of different ways to do this, but here are three really common and really effective ones:

- **Switch the timeframe:** If you made your verses different chronologically – like by talking about a first and second date – then use the bridge to take us to or talk about a different time period again. So you could talk about the past – how lonely your singer's life was before they met this person – or jump into the future – what they think their life might be like together in the immediate or more distant future.

- **Zoom out in perspective:** Some songs really benefit from a broader or more philosophical take on their main idea or thesis. So if your song is about someone who's suffering the pain of a specific heartbreak, in the bridge you could talk about heartbreak more generally – like 'Sometimes hearts get broken…', or 'It's true, love hurts…', or 'Love's a game and sometimes you lose…'. You usually want to be careful about making any of your song lyric too general – as you know, specifics bring song lyrics to life – but in your bridge, something more general that adds some context or a fresh perspective to your song's specific situation can work really well.

- **Reject an opposite perspective:** If you try to argue a point seriously, one common and really persuasive technique is to take an opposite perspective and show it as flawed or wrong somehow. Sure, a song isn't a court case, but this idea also works great in a song's bridge – in short, you bring up some opposite perspective or angle then say or show that that perspective isn't really true or doesn't matter. So if your song's message is 'Hey world, I'm back', you could write a bridge that says 'Some people thought I was gone for good, but look how wrong they were'. Or, if your song's message is 'Everyone should love each other', in the bridge you could talk about some of the negative consequences if we don't.

So have a think about what might work in your song – because bridge lyrics are all about this kind of fresh perspective or angle of attack. You might find your song works perfectly with one of these three techniques, or one of those ideas might spark some other idea that sounds promising.

Either way, like always, it's often worth brainstorming a handful of different approaches that could work. (Most song ideas have tons of fresh perspectives you could use to write a bridge.) Then after that, you can pick out the approach you like most. And once you've settled on a lyric perspective that works, you can start work on the actual lyric.

Write the Bridge Lyric

When it comes to writing the actual bridge lyric, the process is basically the same as the one you used to write your song's verses – so by now you're no doubt a pro at it.

But like before, you'll want to spend some time coming up with different ideas, phrases and rhymes that explore your bridge's overall focus. Then you can craft those ideas into a finished bridge lyric.

It's a good idea to keep your bridge lyric either the same length as your other sections – so probably eight lines – or try something shorter – like maybe four lines. Like always, you want your song sections to feel mostly balanced in length, but sometimes – especially in a lighter or less intense bridge – something shorter can work really nicely. (Though whatever you pick, if your song has generally been two measures for each lyric line, it's a good idea to maintain that in your bridge.)

It's also a good idea to stick to a simple rhyme scheme again in your bridge. But still, because the purpose of your bridge is to take us somewhere new, you can try something a bit different if you like – including not rhyming at all.

Finally, a great way to approach writing a bridge lyric is to figure out a final line to aim for and then work backwards – or write your first and last lyric lines and then try to connect them.

In fact, that's especially true in a song's bridge because the final lyric line of the bridge is often especially important – it's often the crux of what the song is *really* about, or what it's saying on a deeper level. So if you came up with an especially strong line that sounds like it goes deep into what you're trying to say in the song, the last line of your bridge is a great place to put it.

But that's basically it. As ever, you want to let your intuition guide you. You want to keep trying different things until you have a bridge lyric that works. And with writing bridges in particular, if what you end up with feels looser or rougher than normal – even like a free, stream-of-consciousness list of ideas – that can work too.

So go ahead. See what you can come up with.

Write the Bridge Chords, Melody and Groove

Like with your bridge's lyric, the job of your bridge's music is to feel fresh and different, but still part of your song's overall world somehow. You're trying to create something that feels like an escape or diversion from your song's 'business as usual'.

That means it's pretty rare to find song bridges that just copy and paste musical ideas from other parts of the song. Still, like with making sure your song's verse and chorus grooves belong together, if there's a musical idea somewhere in your song you can use to inspire your bridge – a rhythm, a melodic shape, an instrumental sound or technique, even a general vibe or feeling – that's often worth taking advantage of.

You've worked through this process at least a couple of times by now, so this time I'll leave it to you to start with either the chords, melody or groove – whichever part you feel most excited about, or whichever part feels like the path of least resistance – and build the rest of your song's bridge from there.

But whatever order you try to do that, let's talk about a few great ways of creating contrast in each element of your bridge.

In your bridge chord progression, think about using chords that take us somewhere new. That doesn't mean you have to throw in the most obscure or random chord you can think of. But that does mean if there's a chord you like but you've not used in your song yet, your bridge is a great time to use it.

Even better, starting your bridge with a different-sounding chord – even if you've used it somewhere else in a minor way – is a great tactic. (That also means the tonic chord, chord I or i, isn't a good choice for the first chord in your bridge – because it sounds too much like home.)

For your bridge vocal melody, what's most important is to write something that works well as a melody in its own right, of course. But if you can find a way to make your bridge melody slightly different somehow, that's even better. Maybe that means introducing a new rhythmic idea you haven't used yet, or including some longer notes if there weren't many before. It's also not uncommon to find the highest note in the song so far in the bridge (so the song's vocal register expands into new territory).

But equally, plenty of bridge melodies aren't that exceptional. If your chord sequence and grooves sound particularly fresh, sometimes a more expected vocal melody on top can work just fine.

With your bridge instrumental groove, you have the most opportunity to conjure up something that sounds creative and new. Again, what's most important is that what you write sounds like it's from the same musical world you've already established in your song, only some part of it you haven't taken us to yet.

Here are a few common and really effective ways of making that happen:

- Add extra parts or layers – like an extra synth or strings track in a DAW, or a more complex piano or guitar part.

- Keep the feel – or the general rhythm – of your song's chorus groove, but transform or reinvent it for your bridge somehow.

- Or, give us a different musical vibe somehow – if your grooves had busy, intense rhythms before, give us something that feels calmer or more static. (But, if you like, you could keep that intensity ticking away gently or quietly somewhere in the musical texture.)

- Either expand the song's register – use instrumental pitches you've not used before – or, alternatively, shrink it so it feels more self-contained. Dropping out the bass, the lowest pitches, is a really common technique for making a bridge feel different or even otherworldly.

- Either lower the **dynamics**, or volume – quiet, 'floaty' bridges can be really effective – or increase the volume to somewhere you haven't been yet – climactic bridges can work well too, depending on the song and your bridge lyric's message.

I know, that's a lot of different options – and as always, not every option will work for every single song. You'll have to try out a few different things to figure out what sounds right within the world of your song. And if you're ever short of inspiration, it's never a bad idea to go listen to some of your favorite songs and figure out how they create contrast in their bridges – and how you can use those techniques in what you create.

And if you were wondering what happens to your song's intensity or energy levels in its bridge – like we talked about in Part 7 – the answer is that there isn't one single answer. Some bridges go much lower in intensity to build back up to the final chorus, while some maintain the intensity of the chorus, only in a different way.

That's because, while you'll want to keep track of what your bridge is doing in terms of intensity and energy, the most important thing with your bridge isn't how exciting or intense it feels, it's how much it takes us somewhere fresh and new. That's why there are a few different intensity 'profiles' or overall plans you can make work.

So there you go – those are the basic principles of writing a good 'standard' bridge.

If you decide to stick with this option, take some time now to write a bridge for your song, add it to your lyric sheet and find some way to record it or write it down, then feel free to skip straight ahead to Part 10.

But if you're considering writing a different kind of bridge – or you're just curious to know what your options are – let's talk about that now.

 ## ADD A BRIDGE

- **Find a contrasting lyric perspective for your bridge – something that explores your song's big idea, but from a fresh angle.**
- **Write a fresh vocal melody, chord progression and groove for your bridge – so your bridge sounds different, like a diversion or an escape.**
- **Alternatively, you could write an instrumental bridge or even no bridge at all.**

TWO OTHER APPROACHES

Writing a 'standard' vocal bridge is an essential songwriting skill and, like I said, the best way to approach bridge if you're new to this process. But now let's look at two other options – writing an instrumental bridge and writing no bridge at all – in case you want to try something a bit different.

Writing an Instrumental Bridge

If the purpose of a song's bridge is to provide contrast, one bold way of taking the song somewhere new is to write a bridge without any vocals at all – an **instrumental bridge**, or just an **instrumental**.

In fact, an instrumental bridge can be a great option if a) your song is quite vocal-heavy or word-heavy and you think it'd benefit from a break in the vocals, or b) you have access to a great performer – maybe a guitarist, pianist or sax player – you really want to showcase in your song.

The truth is, instrumental sections can happen at a handful of different points in a verse-chorus song, but just like with a vocal bridge, the spot just after your second chorus where your structure might otherwise start to feel predictable is a really common location.

With an instrumental bridge, you can be as creative as your imagination will let you, but here are a few important things to bear in mind:

- Most instrumental bridges make one or more instruments the focus of the section – they're not just grooves on their own. Guitar solos and synth solos are really common in rock and pop songs – and you have the option of writing something specific, or, if your song will be performed live, of asking your performer to improvise over a particular chord progression.

- That said – and especially if you're producing with a DAW – some instrumental grooves don't necessarily feature a solo instrument. But they usually compensate for that by making sure their grooves are extra interesting and attention-grabbing – so that the instrumental parts really become the musical focus.

- Some instrumental bridges are completely original, but some, like we've spoken about before, are based on some other part of the song. Sometimes they'll use a chord progression from somewhere else in the song. Sometimes, even though they're a bridge, they'll actually be a repeat of the verse – either just with the verse chords, or a with version of the verse melody played on an instrument.

- One other good option is a hybrid bridge – a bridge that has both a lead vocal and one or more featured instrumental parts. Maybe the vocal and instrumental solos weave around each other, or maybe the instrumental solo takes the lead while the vocal does some riffing, or adds some 'ooh's and 'aah's, or repeats some fragments of the chorus melody or lyric somehow. As long as this feels like a break from the norm – like any bridge should – it can be really effective.

- Writing an instrumental bridge gives you plenty of freedom to write pretty much whatever you like, but it's usually worth keeping this section roughly the same length as your other main sections – so probably something like 16 measures, give or take.

Like always, what works in one song won't necessarily work in every song – so you'll have to use your judgment to decide what fits.

But if you think an instrumental bridge is a good choice for your song, have a play around and see what sounds good. Go find an instrumental escape or contrast that takes your audience away for a while before you bring them home to the final chorus.

When Not to Include a Bridge

Finally, you might be wondering whether every song needs a bridge. Are there songs that are better off without them at all?

And absolutely – bridges are completely optional. A lot of songs have them, but that doesn't mean every song has to.

The main reason – really, the only reason – to add a vocal bridge is because you think adding a different perspective will really enhance or deepen your song's message. After a good vocal bridge, you land back in the song's chorus, but it's different somehow. The bridge has shifted how we understand and appreciate the song's overall message.

Ditto, the main reason to add an instrumental bridge is because you think adding a breather or a break – or just a focus on a particular instrumental solo – will add to your song somehow. A good instrumental bridge takes us away from the main body of your song and helps us appreciate it all the more when it comes back in the final chorus.

So if your song doesn't need either of those things, maybe it would be better *without* a bridge. Maybe your song's verses and choruses are giving your song everything it needs already.

If you're a highway engineer, you only build a bridge when you have two points to connect over a valley or river. And if you're a songwriter, you only really need a bridge when there's some kind of musical or lyrical gap that's worth bridging too.

And if that sounds like the song you're working on, there's nothing wrong with finishing with a third chorus – or the chorus twice over in a 'double' chorus – and calling it a day.

There's a saying in songwriting – well, all art really – that content dictates form. In other words, what you have to say helps you decide how you say it. And while it would be really weird to write a verse-chorus structure without a verse or chorus, when you start to play with some of the other sections, they're strictly optional. Whether you include them or not comes down to whether they have a place – whether they're worth including – in your song.

And if that means no bridge, sometimes that's the perfect choice.

OK, so there we are. Spend a moment mulling over the options we've talked about to decide what's best for your song. Then, if you decide to include a bridge, have a play around until you come up with something that feels right for the message and vibe of your song overall.

And once you're done, make sure you add it to your song's lyric sheet. If you opted for an instrumental bridge, adding 'INSTRUMENTAL (16 measures)' to your lyric sheet is always worth doing – so your song's structure is clear. And whatever kind of bridge you write, don't forget to make sure you have a record of its music one way or another.

Then we'll move on to two more useful but optional sections in Part 10 – your song's intro and outro.

[PART 10]
ADD AN INTRO AND OUTRO

[PART 10]

ADD AN INTRO AND OUTRO

In this part... / How to complete your song
with an effective intro and
outro.

Alrighty. You're almost done. All that's left is to figure out how to start and finish your song – how to add an effective intro and outro.

Like in the last part, I'm going to give you a few different ways to do that. And also like in the last part, if you're new to this process I recommend you stick with the most straightforward options – but if you want to write something a bit more adventurous, I'll give you a couple of more advanced techniques you can try instead.

ADD AN INTRO

Intros are usually very important – and most songs have them. Their job is simple: to set up the musical world of your song before your singer comes in, and if your song's going to be performed live, to give your singer the song's key, tempo and vibe before they start to sing.

Let's start with probably the simplest – and most common – way to do that.

The Simplest Way to Add an Intro

A really common and effective way to give your song an intro is just to extend the beginning of your first verse's groove back a few measures. In other words, whatever the non-vocal parts do at the beginning of your first verse, you copy and paste that an extra time before your verse begins:

This technique lets us get familiar with your first verse's groove before the vocal is added. It's a simple trick – but it tends to work really well.

The most common way of creating this kind of intro is to repeat the first four measures of your first verse's groove – especially if it has a repeating four-chord progression, like in my example. Sometimes a two-measure intro works better, or an eight-measure intro, or even just a one-measure intro – but four is often the magic number. So it's worth playing around to see what's right for your song – and what's long enough to help your audience and singer settle into the tempo, key and feel your song before it starts for real.

If you want to vary this basic format a bit, you could have your singer do some vocal riffing during your intro. Or you could have them drop their name a couple of times so we know who's performing on the track. (Shout out to you, Jason Derulo.) Or, if you're writing in a DAW, you might want to add an extra instrumental layer – like a short guitar melody – especially if your verse groove feels too plain.

But you get the idea – extending your first verse groove back a few measures is a really simple but effective way of creating an intro.

Two More Advanced Ways to Add an Intro

Alternatively, if you want to try something a bit more advanced – either because you fancy a challenge or because you're not sure the simple groove-extending technique is right for this particular song – let's talk about two other ways of creating an effective intro:

- **Add a 'preview' chorus:** One way a handful of commercial pop songs create an intro is by including an extra chorus *before* the first verse. That might sound weird, but it's a neat way of getting your listener familiar with your chorus before it comes in for real later on. If you do that, one way you can make sure the preview chorus doesn't take away from the moment your first full chorus hits is to thin out the preview chorus's texture somehow – maybe take out an instrument or a big chunk of the vocals – so it feels like a warm-up or preview of the real thing. A great real-life example of this type of intro is in Ariana Grande's 'no tears left to cry'.

- **Write a composed introduction:** If you feel up for it, you could try writing an 'original' or composed introduction instead. Usually, 'original' intros are similar to what comes next somehow – you want it to sound like it's from the same song – so it might use similar sounds, or your verse's chord progression, or an idea from some other part of your song. But however you do it, your goal is still to ease us into the main body of your song. (A really extreme example of this idea is Michael Jackson's 'Thriller' – which famously starts with a long, original intro before the main groove comes in. But for something more typical you could check out 'Let's Get It Started' by The Black Eyed Peas – which starts with a big vocal riff then an original intro based on the song's main chord progression – and Charlie Puth's 'Through It All' – which starts with a piano solo intro based on the last eight measures of the chorus.)

I gave you a handful of specific examples just now, but there are lots of subtly different ways to make these types of intros work. So if you want to explore what else is possible, it's always a good idea to go listen to some of your favorite songs to hear how their intros work – and how you can use those techniques yourself.

Like bridges, intros are technically optional – and some songs have intros that are so short that you might wonder whether they count as proper intros at all. But even if you decide your song doesn't need much of an intro, part of writing any song is making sure you ease us into it in a satisfying way, so you'll want to be sure you're happy with the way your song goes from 0:00 to the start your first verse.

ADD AN INTRO

- **Find a neat way to start your song before your singer comes in – maybe by extending your first verse groove back a few measures, introducing a 'preview' chorus, or by coming up with something original.**

ADD AN OUTRO

Similarly, once you've figured out how your song is going to start, you'll want to figure out how it's going to end.

Sometimes ending your song is as simple as rounding off the final chorus by landing on a clean held chord. But often you'll want to write a short, dedicated section – an outro, or ending – to bring your song to a close.

So now, let's look at three common ways to finish off your song. This time there are two simple ones – which, again, are great choices if you're new to this – plus a more advanced one if you want to try it.

Two Simple Ways to Add an Outro

One really simple way to end your song is to tweak the ending of your last chorus somehow so it feels final, like it comes to rest. A few common techniques songwriters use to do that include:

- Changing the chorus's final measure so the groove lands on a long, held chord.

- Changing the end of the chorus so it cuts off in a clean or satisfying way.

- Changing the end of the chorus so it finishes with a mini flourish or 'button' – like an accented chord, or a final-sounding two- or three-note idea (a 'duh-duh' or 'duh-duh-duh').

- Adding a **ritardando** – a slight slowdown – up to the final note.

- Adapting the end of the chorus so it lands on the tonic chord (chord I or i).

Sometimes you'll find you can use two or more of these techniques in combination. And sometimes you'll want to add a measure or two to make these ending types work, though occasionally you can just tweak the final measure to create a satisfying ending.

Here's one example, that adds a couple of extra measures by continuing the groove a bit, before finishing the song off with a clean and final three-note idea (one of those 'duh-duh-duh's I was talking about):

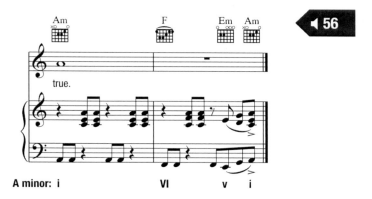

And here's another, where the regular Em–C–G–D chord progression goes directly to the tonic chord, G, in the last measure to bring the song to a close, with a quick ritardando (the 'rit.') to make it sound extra final:

These two examples are so simple that they don't really give you an 'outro' section – just an adapted final chorus. Some of the other options, though, might mean adding a few measures to make them work – and that's fine too. What's most important, as always, is that you play around to figure out what sounds right for your particular song.

The second really simple way to end your song is to write what's called a 'repeat and fade'. As you can probably guess, that means you repeat the chorus an extra time and have it gradually fade out to zero volume. That makes a repeat and fade an ideal choice if you're writing in a DAW – though live performers sometimes get asked to create this effect too.

So try a few of these options and see what you think. As usual, they won't all work for every song. But as usual, the best way to find out what will work for your song is to try some things out and see what sounds good to you.

One More Advanced Way to Add an Outro

And finally, if you're feeling more adventurous, you could write an original 'composed' outro – just like writing a composed intro – if you like. This kind of outro is sometimes called a **coda**, which is a more traditional term for a piece of music's ending.

And again – just like with composed intros – most composed outros are based on some of the musical ideas that already exist in the song.

So, for example, Rudimental and Jess Glynne's 'These Days' adds a quick coda by repeating last line of the chorus – "We wish we could come back to these days, these days' – an extra time in a more *a cappella* (unaccompanied) style to wind the song down. Ed Sheeran's 'Thinking Out Loud' does the same thing but with the last line of the chorus *two* extra times – with a few subtle changes each time. That kind of simple repetition is a really common way to finish a song.

Most songs being written right now have fairly short outros, but for songs with longer composed outros you can check out Stevie Wonder's 'I Wish', The Buggles' 'Video Killed the Radio Star' or – for a more recent example – 'Uptown Funk' by Mark Ronson and Bruno Mars.

There are tons of great ways to write a composed outro by taking an existing part of the song and doing something new with it. So if you want some inspiration, it's a good idea to go listen to your favorite songs – or some of my examples – and you'll find plenty of ideas.

ADD AN OUTRO

- **Find a way of rounding off your song – maybe with a held chord, a clean cut, a 'repeat and fade' or an original 'composed' ending.**

And at long last, that's it – all ten parts done and this process fully completed.

In the next section – which I've called the book's outro – we'll round off with a few ideas for what you can do next to keep writing and keep growing as a songwriter. But before we do that, you'll want to make sure you've put your finished song together.

First, if you need to update your lyric sheet, go ahead. (Lyric sheets usually include the lyrics in song's intro and outro if they have any singing in them – but if yours don't it's fine not to mention them on your lyric sheet.)

Then you'll want to make sure you end up with a complete recording, score, or project file for your song – however you've been keeping track.

And then you're done – that's it. So it's time to pat yourself on the back and figure out where you go from here.

[OUTRO]
CONGRATS — AND
WHAT'S NEXT

[OUTRO]
CONGRATS — AND WHAT'S NEXT

In this part... | *A moment to celebrate the song you just finished – plus, where you can go from here.*

Congratulations! **You finished an entire song.**

Maybe that sounds over the top, but honestly, it's a big deal.

You created something out of nothing. You turned a blank space into a finished song. You created something that's never existed before, in your own way, on your own terms.

And what's more, you jumped fearlessly into a ton of new songwriting ideas and techniques – and that's a big deal too.

So take a bow. Take a breather. Take the rest of the week off if you like.

And after that, if you're wondering what you can do next to keep going and take on a new challenge or two, let's talk about some of your options.

Write Something New

If you've just finished one song, starting a new one might be the last thing on your mind right now. But once you're ready, you'll definitely get a whole lot more out of working through this process all over again.

That, honestly, is the best thing about working through a process that isn't a formula or method – you can go through it as many times as you like and always get different results.

And as I said in the introduction, the more you work through the process, the more it will change – the more you'll learn about songwriting, the more you'll understand which parts of the process are negotiable and which aren't, and the more confident you'll become at writing in your own style and in your own way.

That's the beauty of songwriting – you never go back to square one. You're always evolving and discovering more about songwriting – and yourself – song after song after song. So knock yourself out.

If this was your first song, it's worth repeating this exact process over again to become more confident with it. But as you get more experienced, you could also try writing the parts of a song in a different order or using this process to finish songs you've already started but never completed. Or, if you want to, you could even try writing some songs with a different structure. (There's more about writing other song forms in *The Art of Songwriting*.)

As you know, it takes time to develop as a songwriter. It takes a few songs before you feel like you've really got a handle on what you're doing. So don't stop now. Keep writing and keep creating new things.

Co-write Something

One great way to go through this process again and get something completely different out of it is to do it with someone else. Every writer has different tastes and experiences, so co-writing is a great way of learning from other songwriters and seeing what creative magic you can rustle up as part of a team.

As I said earlier in the book, if you co-write this time it's important to decide how you're going to split up the writing process — whether one of you focuses on music, one of you on lyrics, or whether you write everything together, or something else entirely. Plus, however you split it up, collaboration is all about conversation — with the right co-writers, bouncing drafts and ideas off of each other will make you all better songwriters than you are alone. So unless you're writing together physically the same space, you'll want to speak regularly as the song comes together.

Of course, if you already worked through this process by co-writing you could try the process over again on your own, or try it with a different co-writer and learn something completely new that way.

You might already know some writers you could approach for a co-write. If not, a local songwriting workshop or online songwriting community is a great place to meet new co-writers, so don't be afraid to put yourself out there.

Get Rewriting

It's a cliché but it's true — great songs aren't written, they're rewritten. No artist does their best work on their first draft, or even their fifth. So if you're serious about writing the best songs you possibly can, rewriting — the art of revising and improving your early drafts — is an essential skill to master.

If you're still new to songwriting, you'll probably benefit most from starting new projects for now – like by repeating this process with a new song idea. Then once you've got a handful of songs under your belt, that's a good time to start thinking about how you can come back to some of your finished songs and see if there are any areas you want to improve.

Rewriting usually happens best at a distance – after you've had some time away from the song, when you can come back to it with a fresh perspective. So if you're thinking about rewriting the song you've just finished, it's a good idea to give it at least a week before you start making any changes. (Though make sure you save your original version somewhere, just in case you decide you like it better after all.)

Rewriting is usually as simple as taking a cold, hard look at what you've created, trying to figure out what's not working the way it could, then trying to polish or tweak those rough edges until they sound better.

Sometimes this is hard work – especially when it comes to being brave enough to replace something that works but is only OK with something that's really great. And honestly, it's a never-ending process – if you look hard enough, you'll always find something more to improve or reconsider, so eventually you reach a point where you have to decide you're done. As the saying goes, a work of art is never finished, only abandoned.

For that reason, it can be tricky balancing quantity – writing lots of songs – and quality – focusing on writing a few great songs. But as I said, if you're new to songwriting, it's usually best to focus on finishing plenty of songs while you learn your craft. Then, as you find your feet, you can spend more time rewriting and revising your most promising projects until they really, really shine.

Check Out Some Other Songwriting Resources

If you're looking for new ideas and perspectives about songwriting, a great place to start is to visit the full reading list I keep on The Song Foundry site at **thesongfoundry.com/bookshelf**. But if you've enjoyed this book, there are three resources I especially recommend for deepening your understanding of how songwriting works.

The first is Austin Kleon's *Steal Like an Artist* – which isn't even about songwriting specifically. The first in a three-part series about creativity, *Steal Like an Artist* talks about how to be more creative, how to be influenced by the artists you love, and how to find your own way as an artist. It's short – you could read it in an afternoon – and it'll probably be one of the most powerful books on creativity you've ever read.

The second is Jack Perricone's *Great Songwriting Techniques* – which is probably the most substantial book out there for exploring specific songwriting techniques in a lot of detail. So if you want dive even deeper into some of the theory and practice around writing melodies, creating chord progressions, writing grooves in specific genres and much more, *Great Songwriting Techniques* is a beast, but it's well worth your time.

And finally, if you want to explore the concepts in this book in more detail, you'll probably enjoy my book *The Art of Songwriting*. I know, I've been dropping its name since the introduction, but if you like the creative and open-ended approach in this book and want to take that to a more advanced level, *The Art of Songwriting* is a great next step.

Alternatively, if you're looking for something more practical to do next, you can check out my series of 30-Day Songwriting Challenges. *The 30-Day Lyric Writing Challenge* and *The 30-Day Creativity Challenge* are ideal for beginners, and *The 30-Day Music Writing Challenge* is ideal for anyone with some basic songwriting experience. There's also *The 30-Day Speed Songwriting Challenge* for more experienced songwriters. They're all practical, month-long bootcamps to help you work on your songwriting skills, in some cases in as little as ten minutes each day.

There's also a ton of free resources on The Song Foundry site – including articles, videos and handouts – at **thesongfoundry.com**. So if you're curious, drop on by and see what you can find.

And there we are. That's the end of this book, this process, and this chapter in your songwriting journey. So thanks for having me along for the ride.

And now – whether this was your first song or not – one of the best things about songwriting is that there's always more to learn and there's always more to write.

So keep going. Keep creating. And keep trying new things.

Maybe what you write will change the world. Maybe what you write will change the world of someone you care about. Or maybe what you write will just change *your* world – and maybe that's amazing too.

Happy writing, my friend.

APPENDIXES

[APPENDIX 1]

21 GREAT SONG IDEAS FOR GETTING STARTED

As we talked about in Part 1, finding a great song idea is a big part of your song's success. So in this Appendix, I've made a quick list of 21 great song concepts that work particularly well for beginner writers.

All of the ideas are simple enough that they're easy to get started with, but universal enough that you'll be able to write about them in your own way. You can either use them exactly as they appear, or modify them if you want to.

I took or adapted all of these ideas from my book *The Ultimate Book of Song Starters*, a collection of 501 powerful but open-ended song ideas that's a great complement to this book if you're looking for specific song ideas to get inspired by.

1	Write a song that says 'I love you'.
2	Write a song that says 'I don't love you anymore'.
3	Write a song that says 'I've never met anyone like you'.
4	Write a song that says 'I'm happy' – and tell us why.
5	Write a song that asks someone what's wrong.
6	Write a song that says 'You let me down' or 'You betrayed me'.
7	Write a song that says 'I need you'.
8	Write a song that says 'I deserve better'.
9	Write a song that says 'I don't want to know'.
10	Write a song that says 'I'm breaking up with you'.
11	Write a song that says 'I want you back'.
12	Write a song that says 'I'm starting a new chapter in my life' – and tell us whether you're happy about that or not.
13	Write a song that says 'Let's party'.
14	Write a song about your biggest hope in life.

15	Write a song about your childhood.
16	Write a song about a complicated kind of love.
17	Write a song about what living a good life means to you.
18	Write a song that makes people laugh.
19	Write a song that makes people think about something.
20	Write a song that motivates people to go after their goals.
21	Write a song that makes people happy.

To turn these song concepts into full song ideas, you'll want to flesh them out like we talked about in Part 1 of this book.

That means deciding:

1) Who is singing?

2) Who are they singing to?

3) What are they trying to say?

[APPENDIX 2]

CHORDS, CHORD NOTES AND GUITAR CHART CHEATSHEETS

In this appendix I've put together a series of quick summaries of the main major and minor chords – including the notes in those chords and how to play them on a keyboard or guitar – you could ever use in a song.

First, I've given you a summary of the six primary and secondary triads in each of the four beginner-friendly keys I talk about in Part 4 – C major, G major, A minor and E minor. You'll have to refer back to Part 4 to understand the theory behind these cheatsheets, but they'll give you a quick reference for which chords you'll use the most in any of these keys.

Then, I've given you a summary of the six primary and secondary triads in each of the twelve common songwriting keys I talk about in Part 4. There are other keys, but these twelve are some of the best and most common keys for songwriting.

And finally, there's a complete list of all twelve major and minor triads – including the notes that make them up and a guitar chart for each chord. I've organized these chords according to the cycle of fifths – the principle in harmony that chords usually sound great when followed by the chord with a root five notes lower – which means you'll find closely-related chords either nearby or in the same position on the opposite page.

C Major – Core Chord Palette

	Chord	Chord Notes	Score Notes	Guitar Chart
I	C major	C E G		C
V	G major	G B D		G
IV	F major	F A C		F
vi	A minor	A C E		Am
ii	D minor	D F A		Dm
iii	E minor	E G B		Em

G Major – Core Chord Palette

	Chord	Chord Notes	Score Notes	Guitar Chart
I	G major	G B D		G
V	D major	D F♯ A		D
IV	C major	C E G		C
vi	E minor	E G B		Em
ii	A minor	A C E		Am
iii	B minor	B D F♯		Bm

A Minor – Core Chord Palette

	Chord	Chord Notes	Score Notes	Guitar Chart
i	A minor	A C E		Am
V / v	E major / E minor*	E G♯ B / E G B		E Em
iv	D minor	D F A		Dm
VI	F major	F A C		F
VII	G major	G B D		G
III	C major	C E G		C

E Minor – Core Chord Palette

	Chord	Chord Notes	Score Notes	Guitar Chart
i	E minor	E G B		Em
V / **v**	B major / B minor*	B D♯ F♯ B D F♯		B Bm
iv	A minor	A C E		Am
VI	C major	C E G		C
VII	D major	D F♯ A		D
III	G major	G B D		G

*Chord V (major) is most common in minor keys, but you can often use chord v (minor) instead.

Common Major Keys – Core Chord Palettes

Key		I	V	IV	vi	ii	iii
C major	-	C	G	F	Am	Dm	Em
D major	2♯	D	A	G	Bm	Em	F♯m
E major	4♯	E	B	A	C♯m	F♯m	G♯m
F major	♭	F	C	B♭	Dm	Gm	Am
G major	♯	G	D	C	Em	Am	Bm
B♭ major	2♭	B♭	F	E♭	Gm	Cm	Dm

The symbols to the right of the key name show how many sharps or flats there are in the key signature of each key when it's notated in a score. So '-' means no sharps or flats, '♯' means one sharp and '2♭' means two flats.

Common Minor Keys – Core Chord Palettes

Key		i	V*	iv	VI	VII	III
A minor	-	Am	E	Dm	F	G	C
B minor	2♯	Bm	F♯	Em	G	A	D
C minor	3♭	Cm	G	Fm	A♭	B♭	E♭
D minor	♭	Dm	A	Gm	B♭	C	F
E minor	♯	Em	B	Am	C	D	G
G minor	2♭	Gm	D	Cm	E♭	F	B♭

*To keep things simple, I've only included chord V (major) – the most common dominant chord used in minor keys – but it's possible to use chord v (the minor chord with the same root note) instead if you want.

All Major Triads – Notes and Guitar Charts

Chord	Chord Notes	Score Notes	Guitar Chart
C major	C E G		C
G major	G B D		G
D major	D F# A		D
A major	A C# E		A
E major	E G# B		E
B major	B D# F#		B
F# major Gb major	F# A# C# Gb Bb Db		F# Gb
Db major	Db F Ab		Db
Ab major	Ab C Eb		Ab
Eb major	Eb G Bb		Eb
Bb major	Bb D F		Bb
F major	F A C		F

All Minor Triads – Notes and Guitar Charts

Chord	Chord Notes	Score Notes	Guitar Chart
A minor	A C E		Am
E minor	E G B		Em
B minor	B D F#		Bm
F# minor	F# A C#		F#m
C# minor	C# E G#		C#m
G# minor	G# B D#		G#m
D# minor Eb minor	D# F# A# Eb Gb Bb		D#m Ebm
Bb minor	Bb Db F		Bbm
F minor	F Ab C		Fm
C minor	C Eb G		Cm
G minor	G Bb D		Gm
D minor	D F A		Dm

[APPENDIX 3]

VERSE-CHORUS STRUCTURE CHEATSHEET

For reasons I explained at beginning of the book, this process walked you through how to write a straightforward verse-chorus structure – the 'core' or archetypal version of the most common structure used today.

And to make sure you have a handy summary of what this structure looks like, I've given you a quick outline of all of the key sections, the order they come in, and what they add to the overall structure.

I've also put together a quick guide to the number of measures you often find in each section. This is just a guide – in real life, the number of measures in each section can vary a lot between different songs – but if in doubt, it's a great blueprint to fall back on. It works on the assumption that you'll need two measures of music for each lyric line, which usually works well for songs in **4/4**, **3/4**, **6/8** and **12/8** in most tempos. Sometimes though, you might need to write double or half the number of measures of music for each lyric line.

If you want to know more about song structure – including more advanced ways to build verse-chorus structures, plus other song forms altogether – there's a lot more information in *The Art of Songwriting*.

VERSE-CHORUS STRUCTURE
The Archetypal Form

INTRO	Sets up world of song, and often **VERSE 1** groove.	
VERSE 1	Lyric introduces song situation or story. Music begins at low intensity and builds.	**BUILD**
CHORUS 1	Lyric hammers home central idea of song. Music is higher in intensity.	**HIGHPOINT**
VERSE 2	Same music as **VERSE 1** but new lyric adds new information. Music builds again.	**BUILD**
CHORUS 2	Same music and lyric as **CHORUS 1**, maybe with some minor changes.	**HIGHPOINT**
BRIDGE	Something contrasting – new lyric and new music.	**ESCAPE / DIVERSION**
CHORUS 3	Familiar return to **CHORUS 1**, maybe with something musical added for the final time.	**RETURN**
OUTRO	Brings song to a satisfying ending.	

Bridges, intros and outros – and even third choruses – are optional.

VERSE-CHORUS STRUCTURE
Common Section Lengths

INTRO	2 / 4 / 8 measures	
VERSE 1	16 measures	8 lyric lines
CHORUS 1	16 measures	8 lyric lines
VERSE 2	16 measures	8 lyric lines
CHORUS 2	16 measures	8 lyric lines
BRIDGE	8 / 16 measures	4 / 8 lyric lines
CHORUS 3	16 measures	8 lyric lines
OUTRO	2 / 4 measures	

Sometimes 2- or 4-measure sections called turnarounds – with no vocal, just groove – are included after some or all of the choruses.

ALSO BY ED BELL

The Ultimate Book of Song Starters

The ultimate collection of 501 powerful and inspiring song ideas – chord ideas, title ideas, song situations and much more – to get you writing quickly.

The Song Foundry 30-Day Challenges

Thirty days of powerful and inspiring songwriting challenges to take your skills to the next level.

The 30-Day Lyric Writing Challenge

The 30-Day Creativity Challenge

The 30-Day Music Writing Challenge

The 30-Day Speed Songwriting Challenge

The Art of Songwriting

A unique and comprehensive guide not just about the craft of songwriting, but also about how to be more creative, how to make your own rules and follow your own path as an artist.

All of these titles are available in paperback and digital editions worldwide. Find out more at **thesongfoundry.com**.

ABOUT ED

Ed Bell is a songwriter, educator, author and entrepreneur.

His creative work is mostly in theatre and film, where he's written songs for Pearl Studio (formerly Oriental DreamWorks) and co-wrote the Kleban Award-winning musical *My 80-Year-Old Boyfriend*.

As an educator, Ed is the author of the bestselling book *The Art of Songwriting* and the popular 30-Day Songwriting Challenges series. Ed created The Song Foundry – one of the Internet's favorite songwriting resource sites – in 2014 and his articles are now read by more than 25,000 songwriters each month. He's taught songwriting at institutions including The Royal Central School of Speech and Drama and Bath Spa University, and written content for *Songwriting Magazine* and *Making Music Magazine*.

Photo: Laura Luc

Ed was born in Yorkshire in the UK in 1987 and educated at Cambridge University and The Royal College of Music in London. When he's not sleeping, he's usually creating something new, traveling or catching up with friends.

edbell.com

THANKS

This book could not have happened without dozens of people who aren't me – and like always, one of the best parts of creating this book was getting a ton of great musicians, creators and friends involved in it.

Thanks to Kaytie Lee and her brilliant copyediting eye, which always makes what I have to say smarter and tighter. Thanks to Charlotte Fleming who meticulously picked up lots of last-minute errors and made this book ready to share with you. Thanks to my incredible, creative friends Richy Hughes and Andrew Simmons whose comments and suggestions improved this book considerably. Thanks again to Andrew and the amazing Amelia Cormack for lending their skills to the downloadable tracks that let you hear this book as well as read it. Thanks to Richa Bargotra for her always excellent work creating the eBook editions of my books.

Thanks to all of the songwriters I've coached one-to-one since 2015, who taught me a lot of what ended up in this book, without even trying. Thanks to everyone in The Song Foundry's insanely global community, who engage with the things I create on the daily – and to the songwriters who've taken the time to tell me how my teaching work has impacted them. Writing is a weird and lonely job, so it's always nice to hear from the people I hoped I was writing for.

And finally, thank you to you, for choosing this book. For becoming part of the community of songwriters who read and get inspired by what I create. And because it's people like you who make my crazy life of making things – and helping other people make things – possible. Thank you, thank you, thank you.

For more tools, ideas and inspiration,

visit **thesongfoundry.com**

INDEX

Anacrusis. *See* Pickup

Anticipation, 102

Beat, 50

Bridges

    'Standard' vocal bridges, 200

    Contrasting lyric perspective, 200

    Creating musical contrast, 205

    Instrumental bridge, 208–10

    When they're optional, 210–11

Cadences, 80–84

Chord functions, 79–86

Chord palettes, 69–73, 242–47

Chord progressions, 74–78

    '1+1+2' progressions, 77

    8-measure progressions, 76

    Four-chord progressions, 75

Chords, 60–63

    Cadences. *See* Cadences

    Chord cheatsheets, 241–50

    Chord functions. *See* Chord
        functions

    Chord V in minor keys, 66, 81

    Diminished chord, 64

    Dominant, 67, 80

    Functional notation, 63–64

    Inverted chords, 120

    Major chord, 62

    Minor chord, 63

    Primary triads, 66–68, 69

    Root position, 120

    Root, third and fifth, 61

    Secondary triads, 68, 69

    Subdominant, 67, 82

Tonic, 67, 79

Coda. *See* Outros

Copyright, 191, 193–95

Co-writing, xxxiv, 229

Cycle of fifths, 85, 241

Diatonic. *See* Scales, Diatonic notes

Downbeat. *See* Rhythm, Downbeat

Dynamics, 176

Energy levels. *See* Verse-chorus
    structure, Intensity levels

Free writing, 147–50

Functional chord notation. *See*
    Chords, Functional notation

Grooves, 108–10

    Capturing a song's mood, 109

    Examples, 110–13

    Repetition, 108, 116–25

    Verse vs. chorus grooves, 135

Half step, 62

Harmony. *See* Chords

Holy Trinity. *See* Songwriting's Holy
    Trinity

Hooks in songwriting, 17

Identities, 34, 39

Instrumental. *See* Bridges,
    Instrumental bridge

Intensity levels. *See* Verse-chorus
    structure, Intensity levels

Intros, 215–19

Key change. *See* Keys, Modulation

Keys, 47–50

    Difference between major and
        minor, 47

Modulation, 47, 132
Lead sheets, 191
Lyric sheets, 188–91
Lyrical hooks, 17–19
  Blending lyrical hooks in, 26
  Hook placements, 26, 28, 40
Lyrics
  A shameless Whitney Houston
    knock-off, 29, 31–33, 36–40
  Brainstorming, 38, 150–54
  Closing lines, 152, 157
  Lyrics and syllables, 89, 99
  Matching first and second verse
    lyrics, 182
  Opening lines, 151, 156
  Pivot lines. See Lyrics, Closing
    lines
  Show don't tell, 166
  Specifics, 164
  Tense and voice, 165
  Verse masterplans. See Verse
    masterplans
  Word stresses, 93
Melisma, 89–90
Melody, 100–105, 169–71
  Fitting with a chord, 101
  Focus notes, 101–2
  Non-chordal notes. See Non-
    chordal notes
  Phrases, 104
  Verse vs. chorus melodies, 170
Meter. See Time Signatures
Middle eight. See Bridges
Modulation. See Keys, Modulation
Motifs, 98, 103–4
  Inversion, 103
Music or lyrics first?, 25

Non-chordal notes, 112
  Auxiliary notes (Neighbor notes),
    116
  Leaning notes, 116
  Passing notes, 116
Non-Chordal Notes, 115–16
Outros, 219–23
Phrases. See Rhythm, Phrases and
  Melody, Phrases
Pickup, 93, 96
Preview choruses, 217
Prosody, 90–91, 91–94
Push. See Anticipation
Range, 105, 106, 176
Register, 171
Release. See Bridges
Rewriting, 41, 99, 103, 105, 186–87,
  229–30
Rhyme, 34–35
  Coming up with rhymes, 36, 154
  Internal rhyme, 159
Rhyme schemes, 33, 35
Rhyme types
  End rhyme, 35
  Identities. See Identities
  Internal rhyme, 35
  Near rhyme, 33, 34
  Perfect rhyme, 33, 34
  Slant rhyme. See Near rhyme
Rhythm
  A joke that might not be
    appropriate for minors, xv
  Basics, 50
  Downbeat, 93, 96, 102
  Phrases, 95
  Rhythmic repetition, 95, 97
Ritardando. See Tempo, Ritardando

Scales, 58–60, 65
  Diatonic notes, 58
  Scale degrees, 59
Semitone. *See* Half step
Song ideas
  21 ideas ready to use, 237–39
  Common song types, 9
  Relating every line in your lyric to your song idea, 27
  Songs tell stories, 8
  The single-sentence 'elevator pitch', 6–7
  The three key questions, 12
Song titles. *See* Lyrical hooks
Songwriting's Holy Trinity, 109
Tempo, 54–56
  Beats per minute, 54

Ritardando, 220
Texture, 176
Time signatures, 50–54
  Common time, 52
  Compound time signatures, 52
Tonality. *See* Keys
Triads. *See* Chords
Turnarounds, 187
Unity in art, 6
Verse masterplans, 142–46
  Common formats, 144
Verse-chorus structure, xxii, 129–30, 251–53
  Intensity levels, 172–77
Vocal range. *See* Range
Vocal run. *See* Melisma
Voice leading, 120

Made in United States
North Haven, CT
11 December 2022